THE
THREE
BUCKET
LEADER

A Simple Framework to Energize Your Employees,
Inspire Your Team, and Fire Up Your Followers

T0361601

KAREN A. GILHOOLY

PostHill
PRESS

A POST HILL PRESS BOOK
ISBN: 979-8-88845-627-9
ISBN (eBook): 979-8-88845-628-6

The Three Bucket Leader:
A Simple Framework to Energize Your Employees, Inspire Your Team, and Fire
Up Your Followers
© 2025 by Karen A. Gilhooly
All Rights Reserved

Cover design by Jim Villaflores

This book, as well as any other Post Hill Press publications, may be purchased in bulk quantities at a special discounted rate. Contact orders@posthillpress.com for more information.

All people, locations, events, and situations are portrayed to the best of the author's memory. While all of the events described are true, many names and identifying details have been changed to protect the privacy of the people involved.

Post Hill Press
New York • Nashville
posthillpress.com

Published in the United States of America
1 2 3 4 5 6 7 8 9 10

To my family, whose unwavering support and encouragement have been the foundation of everything I've accomplished.

And to the thousands of colleagues, managers, and leaders I've had the privilege to work with—each of you has shaped my journey, fueled my passion, and inspired the stories and insights within these pages. Thank you for the lessons, the shared visions, and the countless moments that made this book possible.

TABLE OF CONTENTS

INTRODUCTION

I still remember the goose bumps when I heard the news. The CEO was summoning me to his office. Me! Account Manager Karen was personally requested in the big office. I'd hardly worked at the bank a year, yet somehow the CEO already knew of me. How? A cosmic alignment of luck? Happenstance? Serendipity? As I stepped into the executive elevator, I could hardly believe it.

Since my first week at his company, I had daydreamed of meeting the mythical Frank Fischer. This larger-than-life founder grew the firm from scrappy start-up to household name with seemingly superhuman will. The stories of his relentless drive were legendary—predawn arrivals, all-night solo strategy sessions, timesheets that doubled the most diligent workers' counts. Even the senior VPs spoke of his accomplishments in hushed, mesmerized tones.

And today, I would stand face-to-face with this business banking titan! My mind raced as the elevator climbed skyward. I could barely contain myself. What wisdom would he impart? Would he share the magical formula he followed to become successful?

But the moment I stepped into his palatial office, my visions of grandeur crashed down.

"Hi, welcome in, uh…" He had to glance down at a piece of paper on his desk. "Ms. Karen!" There was no gleam of recognition in his eyes. He gestured toward the chair in front of his desk, and before I was fully seated he started a well-rehearsed monologue.

This meeting wasn't a special coaching session, nor was it the start of a conveyor belt leading up to the elusive C-suite. This was simply a mandatory meet-and-greet for random new recruits. Frank Fischer had no particular interest in me, my skills, or my career.

My excitement fizzled out by the time he finished his spiel. I felt woozy with an energy hangover. What had he even said?

"Do you have any questions for me?" he asked.

I had a thousand. Right under my arm was the result of the previous night's frenzy: a notebook full of questions. Now, though, they all felt wrong—naive, maybe. I was embarrassed to think he'd ever wanted to share the secrets of his success with me. I was only a check in a box, a name on a list made for crossing out. What questions could I possibly ask?

"No, sir," I said quietly. "Thank you for your time."

Crestfallen, I turned to leave, but Frank must have noticed my disappointment. Just as I reached the door—

"Karen."

I turned back. There was a sly grin on his face.

"Do you want to know how I got so successful?"

This perked me up. I nodded eagerly, stepping back toward his executive desk. He waited until I was right across from him, then leaned over the desk as if to share his most precious secret.

"Here it is: when it comes to your work, always be in. Never be out."

His words hung in the air, their simplicity belying the depth of their meaning. At first glance, the mantra seemed too straightforward to be the key to his success. If it was that easy, wouldn't everyone follow this advice? But as I mulled over his words, I began to sense that there was more to this simple phrase than met the eye.

Once again, I deflated like a popped balloon. That...was it? The secret to his empire? I found it hard to believe any successful business tycoon's mantra could fit inside a fortune cookie. If it was that simple, wouldn't everyone do it?

Confused, defeated, and a little frustrated, I staggered out of his office. I went through the rest of my day with a chip on my shoulder and a splitting headache. I'd never felt so... disenchanted.

As I reflected on my meeting with Frank, I couldn't shake the feeling that I was missing something important. At the time, the word "engagement" was nothing more than a buzzword buried in corporate memos. No one seemed concerned about whether people enjoyed their jobs or not. As long as the paychecks came every two weeks, the work was worth doing. Those who suffered from a lack of enthusiasm were perceived as lazy, rather than desperately yearning for inspiration and connection.

Similarly, a person's "purpose" was abstract. Fulfillment was for successful celebrities like Meryl Streep and Jack Nicholson, not account managers or customer service reps. Our "purpose" came from our responsibilities, not the other way around. We worked the job, cleaned the home, raised the kids, paid the bills, went to bed, and did it all again the next day. If we wanted more than that—something that actually engaged our interests—we were delusional.

What I didn't realize then was that Frank Fischer's mantra, simple as it was, was true. He knew the value of engagement. Always being in, and never being out, was at the forefront of his mind throughout his career. Consequently, his decisions came from a place of purpose, fulfillment, and personal meaning. He lived his life to its fullest, and if his next potential move didn't engage him, he chose a different path.

It took me years to learn the value in Frank's words. Eventually, I understood the importance of engagement and how it impacts our lives. This book shares stories and frameworks that explain engagement, its significance, and strategies to stay engaged.

Time is our most valuable resource, and disengagement wastes it. If we want to make the most of our time in this life, we must be fully engaged. All in. To that end, what follows is my time-tested advice.

And like Frank's advice, mine is also deceptively simple.

It all starts with a bucket.

PART ONE

The Disengagement Problem

CHAPTER 1

Three Buckets

"I don't know if I can do this again," Michael said.

We stood on the balcony of an office building, backed against the Chicago skyline. My heart still raced from the throes of the strategy meeting. I imagined Michael's heart was racing too, but he hid his discomfort with a long drag on his cigarette.

The summer wind whipped around us, tossing the curls of my hair into limbo. But whatever mess threatened my hair, it was nothing compared to the upheaval facing Michael and his team. A decision had to be made.

This was my last chance to get through to Michael. Our department was in deep trouble, and the man standing across from me was at the heart of all the problems. The bank was out of patience, which meant I was out of time.

I was the go-to woman for one of the world's largest banks' thorniest problems. Over the years, I'd earned a reputation as "the engagement expert," coaxing dozens of employees out of workplace malaise. But Michael would prove a singular case, the first in years to impart a pivotal lesson that altered the course of my career.

My role was that of an engagement paramedic. I was air-dropped into flailing departments to resuscitate flatlining projects. The formula seldom wavered: identify the diseased elements, revive morale with an adrenaline shot of vision, then build momentum with a long string of early wins.

Every time I turned sure defeat into victory, I felt a physical rush. New challenges caused my mind to thrum. I loved diagnosing dysfunction and curing it with strategies for engagement. Time and again I silenced the doubters, winning over the banking industry's weary and skeptical souls.

My engagement elixir was distilled from equal parts psychology, persuasion, and chutzpah. After a series of Hail Mary successes, my methods grew celebrated. I became the emergency specialist on speed dial whenever leadership needed to pull a Lazarus.

This wild ride took me through almost every facet of my organization, where I developed a graduate-level understanding of its inner workings. I turned around software teams, sales teams, analytics teams, customer service teams, and management teams in almost every city from Detroit to Albuquerque to Tucson. In over two decades, I never came up against a problem I couldn't fix...until Michael.

At his prime, Michael was *the guy*. The North Star of his division. A model leader who set a stellar example for up-and-comers. But the years of grinding away at his job had dimmed his guiding light to a small flicker. Now, on that fateful day in Chicago, my entire engagement tool kit couldn't break through his indifference. He might have been a star once, but he was a black hole now, swallowing up all motivation from himself and from his team.

Throughout the strategy meeting, Michael countered my every idea with grunts or shrugs, retreating further into himself. Now on the balcony, cigarette in hand, he spoke words that shook me to my core. "I've been grappling with this decision for a long time, and I just don't know if this job is worth it to me anymore." His shoulders sagged, and my pulse quickened.

My self-doubt turned to panic as a terrifying question gripped me. *If my beloved methods can't spark Michael, how many people had I truly helped before?* How long had I operated on illusion alone? On temporary feel-good adrenaline shots? For the first time in memory, the prospect of real failure stood before me, and I powerlessly stared back.

"What do you mean the job's not worth it?" I stammered. "Michael! You're the guy! You're the one who built out our global franchise, who never took no for an answer, who moved mountains and got it done!"

"That guy doesn't exist anymore, Karen," Michael snarled. He pointed his thumbs toward his chest and shouted, "This is the guy. And I need you to take a good, long, hard look at this guy, because this is what's left of him now."

I winced as I recalled my declaration (loud and proud) to the CEO that I could turn Michael and his team around before the end of the quarter using my Two Bucket system. This promise came with a degree of risk. If I couldn't pull it off, I'd have no choice but to return to headquarters defeated. The CEO specifically selected me for this assignment because of my previous success in similar situations. There was no way I could walk back into his office and tell him I missed the mark. Failure would not be accepted.

Michael's department was bleeding over half a million dollars in lost business every month—a hemorrhage that threatened both our jobs if left unchecked. My idea to host this expensive, high-profile Chicago meeting with Michael and four other senior executives hadn't moved the needle. The air thickened with unspoken ultimatums, and our suite transformed into a pressure cooker set to blow.

I looked over the low clouds stretching off into the distance. As we stood in silence, I took a moment to consider my next move. Behind us, through the glass doors of the conference room, I knew the rest of the management team was watching to see what would happen in the next sixty seconds. I felt the last twenty years of my life compress into a single point, filling my body with a surge of energy. My heart thudded in my throat as my mind reeled. I knew I had to change tack, or risk losing everything.

"Let's look at this a little differently," I started. "Imagine two buckets. One is labeled 'Engaged' and the other, 'Disengaged.' Every time a Minute—that's capital M, Minute—goes by, you get a single coin to represent those sixty seconds. It's a Minute coin. And you have to toss it into one bucket or the other. When I look at you, I see someone who is throwing all his Minutes into the Disengaged bucket. You're spending all your time checked out, Michael. But it doesn't have to be that way. Every sixty seconds, you have the power to make a new choice. You can Engage."

Michael lowered his cigarette and looked at me. "I was engaged, Karen. I spent every Minute for twenty-two years *engaged*. I gave this place my blood, sweat…everything." He paused to take a drag.

"And what did I gain from it all? My wife left me, my kids won't speak to me. I'm a wreck, having spent more time living in hotels than in the comfort of my own home."

He laughed mirthlessly, a hollow sound as empty and desolate as a gust of wind whistling across a wasteland. "So you'll have to forgive my lack of enthusiasm now. I've got nothing left to give to this job or any other. I'm running on fumes in a race that never ends."

He frowned, and then continued. "You don't need to talk to me about the Engaged bucket, Karen. I've lived that dream—and it's damn expensive. I've finally got my life back together, and I don't know if I can go down that road again. I don't think I want it. I wouldn't say I'm disengaged, I'm just…numb."

I flashed back to the old Michael—the poster child for engagement from seasons past. This was the man who tackled eighteen-month postings in Southeast Asia with zeal. Back when his job and identity intertwined, Michael brought teams back from the brink for sport, transforming one after another into well-oiled machines. We had crossed paths in those early days and later lost touch as careers diverged, only to reunite years later.

At first, I failed to reconcile the hollow ghost beside me with the passionate firebrand I once knew. The one who grinned through grueling journeys abroad, fueled by purpose rather than paychecks. As the years passed, his work slowly devoured his identity, consuming him from within like a ravenous beast. The job became his sole purpose, his reason for existence, until it had thoroughly digested every last morsel of his former self, leaving behind nothing but an empty husk, a mere shadow of the man he used to be.

What happened? I wondered, sizing up the specter of my friend standing with me now. How did he lose everything—his family, his friends, and his fire—in a few short years? It was like his Minutes weren't working for him, no matter which bucket he spent them in.

At that moment, something clicked for me.

"Actually," I said, "I think I've got it all wrong. You're not engaged or disengaged. You're in the middle. You're trying to make up your mind which direction you want to go. There aren't just two buckets, there's a third bucket too, in between the others. And you've been throwing your Minutes in there for quite some time."

Michael inhaled deeply, drawing the cigarette smoke into his lungs once more. In the evening light, he looked almost black and white, like a film star from the 1940s. He exhaled little rings of smoke and gazed over my shoulder, toward the Loop and the dark void of Lake Michigan beyond.

"Yeah." He nodded. "Sure."

We stood still for a moment, not talking, watching the smoke from Michael's dwindling cigarette coil around us like a shroud.

I broke the silence. "Michael, it's time to pick a lane. Either commit fully to Bucket One and I'll move heaven and earth to help you recapture your former glory. Or if your heart's no longer in it—and you'll acknowledge Bucket Three—I'll tap every connection I have to ensure you a safe landing somewhere new." I locked eyes with him. "No more limbo. No more living in Bucket Two. No more going through the motions on autopilot. If this work still excites you, I'm ready to do what I can to support you. But if it's time to turn the page, let's start planning your next chapter."

I leaned in, my voice gentle but firm. "The only wrong choice is choosing nothing. So where does your gut say you belong—All In or All Out?"

A painful moment passed as Michael brooded. Then I saw his shoulders straighten. He lifted his chin from his chest and turned toward me. For the first time in months, I saw a sharpness in his gaze as he looked me dead in the eye.

"All right, Karen," he said confidently. "I'm out."

Dammit! I stifled a gasp. It was like he'd punched the wind out of me. But I knew he meant it. There was no changing his mind.

I nodded. "Okay. Let's do it, then."

Over the next few weeks, I worked with Michael on his transition out of the organization. At first, there was a fair amount of pushback. This was *not* the solution anyone had in mind. Michael was the heart of the team! How would they exist without him?

Remarkably, as we approached the final day of our transition, the team's productivity surged threefold. It was as if Michael's apathy had been a contagious virus, infecting the entire team. With his impending departure, the remaining four managers swiftly shed their indifference. Freed from the chains of stagnation, their performance soared to new heights.

A revelation dawned——I had been treating the symptoms of inertia while allowing the real disease to spread like wildfire. No more. For years, I had played the role of engagement paramedic, so focused on reviving individuals that I failed to diagnose the root cause of the problem.

The Binary Illusion

The way most leaders think about engagement is misguided, and I used to be one of them. Before talking to Michael on that brisk Chicago evening, I didn't realize my own mistake. I didn't believe in limbo. I was stuck thinking of engagement as a binary solution: you're either All In or All Out. By ignoring the people who weren't either—who didn't feel motivated enough to choose—I missed a crucial variable.

The human tendency to view engagement in binary terms is nothing new. It's a phenomenon that isn't limited to engagement, or even the workplace. The human brain loves a good sorting system, and a "one or the other" solution is mathematically the easiest. If one person is tall, the next is short. If I'm fat, you're skinny. Not conservative? You must be liberal. Not smart? You've got to be dumb. Binary categories are straightforward, but they're not a reflection of reality. The world isn't as simple as black or white. It operates in shades of gray.

Leaders who succumb to the Binary Illusion, as I did for the first decade of my career, view team members as either engaged or disengaged. This makes the objective seem clear: move the latter to the former. Drag the ones who are disengaged out from the dark side and help them see the light. If only it were that simple.

The complications appear when the majority of the team is neither engaged nor disengaged. We can look at this issue as a bell curve, where most people's level of engagement is charted as a cluster in the middle, but a few hang out on either end. There's a reason statisticians refer to this as a "normal distribution." The curve projects how people fall on virtually every type of measurement, from weight, to height, to intelligence, to income, to political views. The binaries only exist as concepts in our minds, but we treat them as definitive rules for the world around us.

There's another key statistical concept to keep in mind here, and that's reversion to the mean. This refers to people's tendency to move toward the average (or mean) on any scale. In stocks, prices and historical returns make their way back to the middle every few years. The world's most successful companies in the 1950s were mediocre by the turn of the century. The skinniest twenty-somethings today will put on more than a few pounds by age forty-five. Watch the outliers on either end of any spectrum, and you'll see them slowly creep toward the middle of the pack.

This means the most engaged people you lead will disengage over time. And the most disengaged people will likely mellow out. No matter where people start, they will all eventually end up in the same place: the middle.

When it comes to engagement, a leader's true adversary isn't the highly motivated individuals who pour their hearts into their work, nor is it the completely disengaged employees who have checked out entirely, although their struggle should not be overlooked. The real threat lies with the vast majority stuck in limbo, perpetually wavering between engagement and apathy, squandering their potential minute by minute.

Most of our employees, students, athletes, and followers are neither fully engaged nor fully disengaged. They're coasting along, tossing their Minutes mindlessly into Bucket Two, unable to decide whether they want to be All In or All Out. When someone ultimately decides they are All Out, they will inevitably part ways with the team, group, or organization. As such, these individuals don't pose a significant challenge for leaders. On the other hand, those who wholeheartedly embrace their roles and go All In are a pleasure to lead. They, too, are not the problem.

People in Bucket One have made a clear choice to be fully engaged, dedicating their time to meaningful pursuits. Those languishing in Bucket Three are struggling through their days, desperately grasping at any chance to escape their current misery. They're frantically scrambling to find a way out, be it through job-hopping or drastic life upheavals. The time spent in Bucket Three is often grueling and demoralizing, as these individuals desperately cling to the faint hope of a less miserable future, all while sacrificing their present well-being in the process.

Bucket Two, the Limbo Bucket, is where Minutes are most often wasted. Many times, people slide into Bucket Two without noticing. They're neither engaged nor disengaged; they're simply coasting along. They take each Minute for granted, thinking, *If I can just get through this, then life will be better.* But without meaningful effort, life doesn't get better. It stays the same, and the Minutes spent waiting are lost.

The biggest threat to a team's success is not the highly engaged or disengaged individuals but the majority stuck in the middle of the bell curve. These people coast along, indifferent and uncommitted, and their apathy can spread like wildfire. As leaders, it's our job to inspire these fence-sitters to choose engagement over indifference and create a culture that encourages everyone to bring their A-game to the field.

The problem is that when we put our Minutes in Bucket Two, it's hard to muster the awareness to pull ourselves out. Most of the time, it takes some impactful event to snap us out of cruise control and force us to rev up (All In, Bucket One) or pull over (All Out, Bucket Three). It's our natural state to coast along, and so nobody—*nobody*—is immune to the magnetic force of Bucket Two.

It Can Happen to Any of Us

For years, I couldn't wrap my head around how people could allow themselves to slip into a never-ending cycle of mediocrity. I used to think the solution was simple: if an activity no longer lights a fire within you, stop wasting your time on it! If you're not investing nearly all your energy into things that truly matter to you, either find a new reason to be passionate about what you're doing or move on to something else entirely.

Oh, how naive I was. It wasn't until my husband took drastic action that I realized even I, the self-proclaimed engagement guru, wasn't immune to sliding back into the middle of the pack.

Life was cruising along smoothly for quite a while. My first-born graduated and embarked on a career in medicine, while my youngest set his sights on becoming a lawyer. My husband settled into retirement, and I found fulfillment in weaving my magic at the bank, keeping me both engaged and content.

At some point, though, I stopped engaging. I don't know when or how it happened. I thought everything was fine, or at least my problems didn't feel overwhelming or all-consuming. My stress was good stress. After all, I'd just been promoted to a new role, and life was going well—if busier than ever. Then…

"You need to talk to Dad."

The same message came from my brothers and sister several times a day. They delivered it through texts, phone calls, and emails. And every time it came, I had the same thought: Why did *I* need to talk to Dad? Couldn't one of them do it? What was so wrong that it needed my attention right now? I had customers to please, employees to lead, and senior executives demanding answers. I was *busy*.

I found myself stretched thin, unable to find the time or energy to have another difficult conversation with my father. My responsibilities at the bank were reaching a breaking point, with my days filled to the brim with complex, high-stakes, and emotionally charged calls. The demands were so relentless that I barely had a moment to catch my breath between meetings. Personal pleasures like my fitness routine, date nights with my husband, weekend gatherings with my children, and most crucially, a full night's sleep, had to be sacrificed. By the time I wrapped up my workday, which often stretched well past the stroke of midnight, I was in no state to engage in any meaningful dialogue. The last thing I wanted to face was a heavy discussion with my dad about his life choices. I was out of gas.

My father was living with a terminal cancer diagnosis. But while his body was ravaged by the disease, his mind remained sharp as a tack. He refused to surrender and spend his remaining time as a victim. He wanted to stay connected with the world for as long as he could.

Other people—primarily my family and the doctors—did not agree with his approach. They felt Dad would be best served by sitting back and conserving whatever energy he had left. They told him he had worked so hard for so long, and he deserved a break.

My father ignored them. Almost in defiance, he tackled a home improvement project that he'd postponed for years: the refurbishment of his computer desk and credenza.

My siblings were concerned about the physical strain associated with this activity. At only eighty-six pounds, Dad spent all day lugging wood, table saws, and other materials up and down the stairs of his house. And at the end of each day there was a sawdusty mess left in his wake. My family didn't get it. What could be the rationale behind remodeling a desk he would never get to use?

Since Dad *clearly* wasn't listening to reason, the family called me in to help restore some "sanity" to the situation. But…I was *just so busy*. I didn't have time to referee a match between my hardheaded siblings and even harder-headed dad.

Weeks went by with the situation unchanged. One morning I shouted at my sister through the phone, "Please, just leave Dad alone!" I was…tightly wound. "There's nothing we can do! Dad's following the beat of his own drummer. He's fine. Now excuse me, I'm late for an update call on my latest work crisis."

I hung up and was about to dial my boss when I heard my husband, Brian, call me from the kitchen.

"Karen"—his voice was calm but firm—"I have dinner reservations for us tonight at seven."

I brushed him off, anxious to get to my next call. "That's great, honey. But you know that I won't be ready to go until much later. This hasn't been a great week."

Brian paused. I could see a dozen cutting responses quivering at the corner of his mouth. Instead of firing them off, though, he kept his cool.

"I know you're busy." He looked at me with a resolute expression. "But you've been busy a lot lately, so I want you to close up shop early tonight so we can enjoy the weekend." I could sense his conviction. He was adamant and nothing would change his mind.

"Fine," I harrumphed. "Dinner at seven."

Evening came before I knew it. At ten to seven, I rushed down the stairs, still on the phone, and tumbled into the car next to Brian. I was on my headset the whole drive and had to cut my team off mid-sentence to hang up and go into the restaurant.

As we walked in, I caught a glimpse of myself in the lobby mirror. My hair was still wet from the shower. My skirt and blouse hadn't romanced an iron in a long while. I was a wreck.

The server greeted us warmly and showed us to our seats. No sooner did my bottom hit the chair than I laid into a rant about my client, my boss, my team, and my work.

"I can't believe we're experiencing these processing delays *again*. Customers are furious. The team is totally out of potential solutions and ideas. Everyone is angry at us for a situation that we didn't create...and we're responsible for managing a message we don't even understand! How much more impossible can things get?"

Throughout the meal, Brian calmly ate his food, drank his wine, and listened to me carry on. I noticed him shifting in his chair a few times and moving his arms at odd angles occasionally. I didn't ask about it—I was too caught up in my tirade. At the end of the meal, he paid the bill and drove me home. I answered a few emails on the drive. Then I dragged myself to bed and closed the book on another awful day.

Despite it being the weekend, the next morning I was on a 5:15 a.m. Zoom call with a team in Europe. I was trying my best to stay focused, but my phone kept alerting me with incessant texts. Ping after ping came from my sister. *You need to talk to Dad, TODAY! He won't take it easy. He's going to hurt himself!* She type-shouted another. *Hello??? Karen??? Call me!*

As soon as my meeting finished, I dialed my sister, exasperated. It was a short call that ended with me fuming and digging in my purse for the car keys.

"Fine," I said through clenched teeth, "I'll go see Dad. Please relax." I rearranged my schedule in my head. *I'll skip my morning workout again and bump the next team callback to 12:30 p.m.*, I thought, grabbing my bag, *but that leaves me on the line until 6:00 p.m. Not ideal, but I'd have time to see Dad, and my sister might dial down the heat a bit.*

Just as I stuck my first foot out the door, Brian called from somewhere in the house.

"*Karen!*"

"What?" I called back. "I'm on my way to see Dad—I need to find out what's going on over there."

"Karen, come here." I followed his voice back to the kitchen. Brian had a strange look on his face. "Sit down. I want to show you something."

"Honey, I—"

"Sit down, Karen. I want to show you something," he said again.

Something in the timbre of his voice warned me this was important, so I walked over to the kitchen table and sat down.

In front of me was my husband's iPad, and on the screen was a video clip. He hit play. It was an edited remix of our dinner conversation from the night before. Brian hadn't been sore or uncomfortable during our meal—it turned out his gestures were signals to the waiter, asking her to record us with his phone.

As I watched the video, I was shocked to see a stranger staring back at me. She wore my clothes and spoke with my voice, but her eyes told a different story. They were sunken, ringed with dark circles, and filled with the same emptiness I had seen in Michael's eyes during our meeting years ago. It was like looking in a mirror and seeing the life drained out of me, just as it had been drained from him. The icy, oppressive force that had consumed Michael now had its grip on me too. I had become a shadow of my former self, a lost soul, just like he had been. As I searched her eyes, desperate to find a glimmer of the warm, engaged person I once was, I found nothing. I was gone, just as the real Michael had disappeared, leaving only a hollow shell behind.

Tears filled my eyes. I slumped down in my chair.

"Is...is that me?" I asked. "Is that who I am?" I looked up from the iPad, my eyes watering.

Brian leaned in, his whisper urgent. "Karen, I've been trying to tell you, but you wouldn't listen. This video was the only way I could show you how bad things have gotten."

Brian's hand gently covered mine across the table, and at his touch, the floodgates opened. Tears streamed down my face as the realization hit me: I had strayed so far from the All In life I had promised myself. This new revelation, combined with the overwhelming pressure of work and the burden of my father's deteriorating health, left me feeling utterly crushed. The weight of it all was suffocating, pressing down on me from every angle, and I felt like I was drowning in a sea of my own broken commitments and mounting responsibilities.

With Brian's words still ringing in my ears and the image of my hollow eyes haunting me, I found myself in the car, driving toward my father's house. Tears streamed down my face, splashing onto the steering wheel as the full weight of my hypocrisy hit me. I was a fraud, a two-faced charlatan who preached one thing but practiced another behind closed doors. At work, I relentlessly pushed my teams to give their all, demanding nothing less than complete dedication or a resignation letter. At home, I instilled in my children the importance of intentionally investing their Minutes in what truly mattered. Yet there I was, oblivious to my own time-spending habits, so consumed by mindless routines that I failed to recognize the gravity of my situation until I saw it mirrored back at me through the shaky footage of a cell phone video. The realization was a gut-wrenching blow, compounding the pain of my father's declining health and the pressure of my work responsibilities.

I was so obsessed with staying engaged at work that I completely missed the fact that I had checked out of my personal life. But here's the kicker: even though I wanted to be All In at work, it was actually sucking the life out of me. It was exhausting, stressful, and totally unrewarding. When you're truly engaged in your work, it should energize you. Every Minute you spend on something meaningful should come back to you tenfold. If I were really putting my Minutes in Bucket One, I'd feel good about where I was. But the truth was staring me right in the face—I was stuck in Bucket Two, and every Minute I spent there was lost forever, disappearing into the void of the past, never to be seen again.

I questioned myself. *How long has this been happening? How long have I despised my job? How long have I been wasting my time?*

The drive to Dad's was short, and I lacked the energy to answer these existential questions before I arrived. It was only 8:30 a.m., and he was already sawing new strips of wood. I heard the shrill of the buzz saw as I walked toward the house. I let myself in and went to the living room, where a cloud of sawdust blurred the image of Dad. He wore his safety glasses and hunched over the noisy tool. He didn't look up but remained focused on the line he was cutting.

Finally, I heard the *clank* of a wood block tumbling to the floor and the whirring down of the saw as he cut the power.

"Dad!" I yelled across the room. "What are you doing?"

"Karen, I know you're here to stop me," he said without taking his goggles off, his gaze fixed on a squat piece of wood. "Don't bother trying. Doctors' orders be damned!"

"Dad," I pleaded. "Would you wait just one minute and talk to me, please?" He set the wood block aside and reached for a two-by-four. "Everyone's worried about you."

He stopped and turned toward me. His chest heaved up and down with an exasperated sigh. He took off his goggles, leaving a pink, swollen ring around his eyes.

"Worried? About what?" He looked at me, and I could see pain lurking in the creases of his face. Oh, his precious face. He was trying to hide it, but the truth was right there—my father was dying, and it hurt. Still, under a layer of pain, sweat, and sawdust, I also saw something else.

Dad was All In.

Mentally, my father was as alive as he had ever been. His eyes shone with determination—the same fierceness I used to see in my own reflection. He was on fire, driven by his purpose. He wasn't going to waste a Minute of whatever life he had left.

"Dad," I said softly, "the doctors told you to rest."

"I don't want to rest," he spat back, a vein bulging in his neck. "I'll rest when I'm dead."

"Yeah, but you might die faster if—"

"Die faster?" My father cut me off. "Come on, Karen, don't you tell me that. Don't tell me to just give up and—"

"I'm not telling you to give up—"

"I will not be a victim of this!" He leaned forward on his table, glaring at me.

I nodded, understanding. Once upon a time, I too approached life with the same fiery determination my father possessed. The stubborn insistence that I spend every Minute in full alignment with my God-given purpose was the basis for my career. But somewhere along the way, for all the fires I helped reignite inside of others, I stopped feeding my own flames. They dwindled and flickered. I didn't even notice when they snuffed out.

It took a wake-up call from my father and husband to finally see just how dark and detached my life had become. I wasn't really living at all—I was just going through the motions, barely surviving on the bare minimum. As I thought back to my conversation with Michael, which felt like a lifetime ago, it suddenly clicked. For the first time, I truly understood how he felt, the weight of his words hitting me like a ton of bricks. I could feel his struggle, his desperation, as if it were my own. It was a painful realization, but one I couldn't ignore any longer.

Michael had seen the real me long before I could. His story wasn't a road map—it was a warning. He recognized in me the same all-consuming work persona that had devoured him, and he knew it was only a matter of time before it swallowed me whole. I shuddered at the thought. Michael had been holding up a mirror, desperately trying to get me to see what he saw, but I had refused to look. Until now.

On my drive home, I called my brothers and my sister. I told them to give Dad space and leave him alone. Let him do what he wants. He's happy, he's not hurting anyone, and it's his life to live. It's *his* time. Those are his Minutes to use, All In or All Out.

The Three Bucket Leader

Picture three buckets: All In, Limbo, and All Out. Every Minute you spend, whether you're leading your team, working on a table saw, or watching television, falls into one of these buckets. But it's not always as straightforward as you might think. Sure, mindlessly scrolling through social media while staring at a screen is probably a waste of your Minutes. But a night spent watching movies with your loved ones? That could be pure Bucket One time. The same goes for using that table saw—if you're cutting wood for a project you're passionate about, those Minutes are more likely to end up in Bucket One than if you're stuck doing endless cuts for a frustrating home renovation.

Unfortunately, simply understanding the Three Bucket model of engagement isn't enough to turn your life—or your team—around. Getting people to recognize they've fallen into the trap of spending Minutes in Bucket Two is a significant challenge. To encourage yourself, your team, your class, or your family to engage in critical self-reflection, you need a clever and creative approach.

Fortunately, I've already done the heavy lifting for you. Throughout my career, I've refined this seemingly simple Three Bucket framework into a comprehensive, step-by-step process that leaders can master. I've discovered the most effective ways to introduce the Buckets to others, guide them in assessing their own engagement levels, and ultimately inspire them to make a conscious choice to invest their Minutes in either Bucket One (Engaged) or Bucket Three (Disengaged).

The system in this book, however, isn't for everyone. Before we dive into the deeper aspects of what it means to be a Three Bucket Leader, there's something you must know first. While this process may seem simple, it's far from easy. This book will challenge you to take a hard look at your own life, both professionally and personally, as well as your physical and emotional well-being.

It's impossible to guide your people through a process you haven't experienced yourself. It's hypocritical to demand a higher level of engagement from your team than you demonstrate in your own life. It's unwise to teach something you have yet to fully embody.

If you're not fully committed to the process, it simply won't work. The title of this book, *The Three Bucket Leader*, isn't just about leading your team through an exercise. It's about living the process yourself if you want it to be effective. Engagement is something you need to fully embrace before you can inspire it in others.

As we conclude this first chapter, the choice is yours. If reading these pages and completing the exercises doesn't ignite a 100 percent commitment right now, set the book aside and return to it when you're ready to fully engage. If this feels like a Bucket Two or Bucket Three activity, one that doesn't align with your passions, don't waste your precious time.

The path ahead demands full fire. Either turn the page with interest…or close the cover and spend your time elsewhere. But choose. The worst betrayal is the one you commit against your own enthusiasm. Your team and your dreams deserve no less than an emphatic yes.

Take a moment right now and think deeply about this. I need you to decide before moving on to the next chapter.

Are you All In or All Out?

CHAPTER 2

The Value of a Minute

For humans, time is our most valuable currency. Yet few of us treat it as such. We fritter it away on mindless distractions, let it slip through our fingers in idle moments, and barter it for money at jobs we despise. But our time is finite. Our Minutes do matter.

How we choose to spend this priceless resource defines us. When we invest our time in people and passions that light us up, we feel most alive. But when we waste time on hollow activities, we drift. And that drifting impacts all areas of our life. If we're disconnected at work, we're likely disconnected at home too. When our most valuable asset is squandered in one place, we tend to squander it in even more places.

Drifting is no way to live. Your time is your life. And you're the only one who can take charge of how you spend it.

The Sears, Roebuck Catalog

When I was a small child, I lived for the Christmas season. To me, Christmas was the most fantastic of holidays, and it began when the Sears, Roebuck catalog arrived in our mailbox. Every year, from the day after Christmas, I couldn't wait for the mailman to deliver it to our door. Until the Sears catalog arrived, I felt like something was missing from my life. Only when the day finally came could I sense the first whiffs of holly jolliness return to my life.

When I was four, I recognized a horrifying pattern: the catalog didn't come until after the last snow of winter melted away. This was problematic because I lived in Chicago, and in Chicago the snow stuck around forever. It could be months past Christmas and the snow would still be sticking around… just to spite me.

I couldn't comprehend the length of the winter season. At the start of each day, I got up and watched the weather report with my mother. Then I religiously waited at my post by the window for the mailman to arrive.

After a few weeks of disappointment and a few temper tantrums, my mother lost her patience. So, she hatched a plan to explain the concept of time to me. A four-year-old.

I was sitting dutifully at the front window when I heard my mother call me into the kitchen.

"Karen," she said, "why don't we look at the calendar together. I want to show you something."

In the kitchen, the calendar was hung by two magnetic strips on the refrigerator. I thought it was just another decoration on the fridge. It was there, and sometimes the image on the top half changed, but the grids, numbers, and tiny notes scribbled in the squares meant nothing to me.

I looked at my mother with a blank expression.

"See this big word at the top? This means we're in the month of March."

I nodded slowly. I'd heard of March. It was a middle-ish time. Not quite winter, but not quite spring. A confusing mix of new flowers and old snow.

Mom took the calendar down and flipped through the pages…one, two, three, four. "Some of the snow is melting now, but we have to wait until this month here, July, for the catalog to come."

I frowned and said, "Oh…okay. We only need to wait for the mailman to come four more times. That's not so bad." I said that last part mostly to convince myself.

"No, honey," Mom said, smiling, "the postman will come lots of times between now and then. See these squares with the numbers on them? Each one of them is a time the postman will come. But we have to wait for this month"—she pointed to July again—"for the catalog."

My heart sank. I couldn't believe it. There were so many squares on the calendar before July! I welled up with tears and crumpled to the kitchen floor, devastated.

"Can't you make it go faster?" I pleaded. "That's so long to wait!"

Then, an even scarier thought occurred to me. "Santa will forget about me by then!"

Mom reached down to me, but I wriggled away from her. I got up and stormed off to my room, mad at her for pretending to teach time when she was actually trying to teach me to *wait*! After a while, she came to my room and sat down beside me on my bed.

"I want to tell you something," she said. I didn't look up at her. I felt betrayed.

"One day you'll understand this," she continued. "Your time is special. You don't want to wish it away. It's much better to find ways to put your time to good use. The catalog will come when it comes, but in the meantime, we have plenty to do."

She gave me a kiss on my forehead and left my room.

Over the next few weeks, I stopped watching the weather. I stopped spending my day hovering at the front window. I spent full days at the local park and the public pool. Before I knew it, my days were so busy that I didn't notice when the last of that year's snow melted away. I had playdates, birthday parties, and field trips to attend. I forgot all about the catalog and the mailman.

Then, as if by magic, I returned home from the park one day to find the catalog sitting squarely in the middle of the kitchen table. It looked just as cheery as I remembered. But seeing it reminded me of my tragic calendar lesson. Months had passed, yet it felt like only yesterday my mother told me about time, and how important it was. Where did all of those Minutes go?

The Geography Book

Years later, in high school, I was sitting in the study hall looking aimlessly around the room. I didn't have anything specific on my mind—my homework was done, I had finished my studying, and I didn't have any books with me. Then, a teacher came up to me and put her hand on my back.

"Karen, you seem pretty fascinated with the walls in this room. They look the same to me as they've always been. What's so interesting that's got your attention?" she asked.

I looked at her and said, "I'm practicing being bored out of my mind."

That didn't go over so well. My teacher's smile was more scolding than amused. "Your beautiful mind is a terrible thing to waste," she gently chided. Then she handed me a geography book from her desk. "Expand your horizons, Karen."

Her simple redirection sparked an aha moment. Just like that, a small dose of inspiration transformed wasted time into opportunity. I was about to learn the power of an open mind and nimble spirit...and a little bit about geography too.

Geography never held my interest, but since that day I've had plenty of time to mull over life's most precious currency. I pondered how best to spend my Minutes, and the choices I made with my time slowly shaped who I became. Just as importantly, those choices shaped how I saw myself.

I learned that wasted time drags the soul, while time spent with intention lifted me up. The determining factor wasn't so much in my ability to always be right in my decision-making but to recognize opportunities to shift gears. Rather than thinking *I'm bored*, I can shift my thinking to meaningful choices. Do I want to be bored, or do I want to be curious? Do I want to be engaged, or do I want to run out the clock? The choices I made shaped my attitude and my time-spending habits.

The Evolution of Minutes

As we age, the value of a Minute evolves. As children, we have little control over how our time is spent. We're prodded awake, pulled through morning routines, then portered off to day care or school. Later we're picked up, brought home, fed dinner, bathed, and put back to bed. Maybe, if we're lucky, there is time to play. In our early days there was little room for independent decision-making. But as the years pass, we have more responsibility over our Minutes.

There comes a day when our Minutes suddenly have value. We realize that we don't *have* to spend it the way we're told. If we want to spend our time with friends, or watching sports, or reading books, or playing video games...we can. We learn how to make decisions with our time, and these decisions begin to form our unique time-spending habits.

Adolescence is a time for learning the value of a Minute. By balancing the competing demands of school, jobs, relationships, and personal identity formation, we learn what is important to us. Except there is a small, teeny tiny problem. During our teenage years, we're absolutely *terrible* at predicting how our daily decisions will affect us years down the road. A neuroscientist might offer a study about how the region of our brain with foresight functionality doesn't fully develop until our mid-twenties, but I'm no neuroscientist. However, can you relate to the feeling that your youth suddenly, one day, slipped away?

By the time our brains are fully developed, we may feel an anxious sense that the "best years" are behind us. But we're still learning how to effectively budget Minutes across all our adult responsibilities. This untimely mismatch between brain development and social timing makes it challenging to take advantage of the meaningful time of young adulthood. Even with a mature perspective, our twenties can seem like a juggling act with too many balls in the air, trying not to drop the ball for work, education, relationships, hobbies, and more. We strive to soak up each Minute before it passes by, but also struggle to prioritize so many competing demands on our time and attention.

Imagine life in the Stone Age—every Minute was consumed with securing the next meal and avoiding imminent danger. As hunters, early humans relentlessly stalked wild game across sweeping savannas. As gatherers, we foraged for berries, roots, and vegetation to stock our stores. Guard duty was nonstop, ever-vigilant against predators and hostile tribes. Over time, innovation afforded us some freedom. Domesticating animals and cultivating crops gave reliable access to food. Building fences and taking shelter in sturdy dwellings helped keep threats at bay. With basic needs met, Minutes became more elastic. But securing survival still dictated daily life.

For our ancestors, Minutes passed in the snapping of twigs and the skinning of deer, untaxed by the luxury of free time or personal fulfillment. Only recently (within the context of all human history) have humans started to question the quality of their time. For all our modern gains, true free time remains out of reach for many. However much we advance, it seems our instinctual desire to jam-pack our Minutes with meaning still makes some of them feel like they're falling short.

As innovation liberated humankind from the worst of its drudgery, Minutes became precious currency. No longer mere units of survival, time wasn't simply passed—it was *spent*. It was a commodity to trade, not just for food and shelter, but for profit and leisure.

As basic survival became more attainable, people earned back some of their Minutes and spent them on pursuits of the mind. Education, personal growth, and social stimulation became the endeavors of those privileged enough to afford them. Each Minute saved by innovation could be invested, stacked, and multiplied. People could build an ever-increasing fortune that contributed to humanity's drive toward modernity.

During the grueling days of the Industrial Revolution, workers endured yearly totals of three thousand labor hours—equivalent to grinding sixty- to seventy-hour weeks for fifty weeks straight. Compared to the modern workforce, the contrast is jarring; today's average employee logs a gentle thirty-five to forty hours across just forty-eight weeks annually. And not only has weekly toil eased but the amount of time we spend alive has shot up: in 1900, average life expectancy languished at only thirty-two years, while today's horizons extend to around seventy-two years.[1] Workers now enjoy both shortened shifts and elongated lifespans, a stark reversal from earlier eras.

For many, having spare time felt strange—like a shiny new toy they hadn't bought but found nonetheless. Without structure, people enjoyed their first few days of play, but the fun wore off and blurred into a hazy boredom. Their interest in the toy dulled, their energy drained, and their inspiration stalled.

These people spent their Minutes wherever they wanted in the moment instead of investing them in their own future satisfaction. The Minutes passed by on TV screens and back porches alike, equal parts gift and burden. Of course it beat scrabbling in the dirt from sunrise to sundown! But they'd traded back-breaking certainty for an unclear horizon. Now time felt precious and precarious, subject to waste if they couldn't puzzle out what mattered most. Each Minute was a choice demanding attention. And it felt like there were so many Minutes in a day now, waiting to be filled.

Freedom granted is not purpose planned. Newfound hours may fritter away, wasted in distraction. Or they might seed the soil for long-deferred dreams, granting time and space to

---

[1] Saloni Dattani et al., "Life Expectancy," Our World in Data, December 28, 2023, https://ourworldindata.org/life-expectancy.

inspire growth. So, with each Minute saved, the great question looms—how to spend it. Will we choose challenge over comfort, inspiration over escape? Or are we doomed to lollygag, hurkle-durkle, and boondoggle while our time slips by?

The Perils of Disengagement

It's easy to forget about one bad day when it's surrounded by good or even average days. It's like forgetting an afternoon rainstorm two weeks after it happened. But when bad days compound, they escalate from a short storm to a hurricane, and the problem gets harder to ignore.

It's easy to write off the occasional disengaged workday as an "off day"—we all have them. But when watching the clock becomes your job's main function, the true problem is a deeper disconnect between how time passes and what makes it meaningful. The danger is resignation—embracing an exhausted, zombie-like trudge as the norm.

What does it mean to be engaged versus disengaged? When you feel engaged, you leap out of bed in the morning as if your mattress were a catapult. The morning sun shines brighter through your windows. The coffee tastes richer. The air smells sweeter. Your emails flow like fine champagne. When true engagement ignites, you'll swear unseen forces are conspiring in your aid. Easy tasks become fluid delight; struggles morph into thrilling experiments. It's as if being fully present unshackles some hidden inner drive that rockets you toward each goal. Time itself seems to pick up your pace as obstacles shift from barriers to mere mile markers. You feel dialed in.

Alternatively, disengagement drags you through days that blur into a lifeless crawl. Each morning you jolt awake to a screeching alarm. You rub your crusty, bleary eyes. You choke down bitter coffee to kick-start the body. The commute creeps by, scenery blending into a monotonous smear of gray. Chipper office greetings elicit inward groans. Seconds tick by like molasses, each Minute an exhausted battle.

The signs seep in slowly—cynicism, then apathy, then grim acceptance. A grinding inertia takes hold within until every task makes you want to rip the hair from your head. Inside, your spark fades and threatens to go out altogether. Each moment exists to pass the time. Without purpose, hours stack up to form faceless years, filled with nothing but the basic truth: yes, this time did pass.

Trapped on the outskirts of your own existence, you watched the world shuffle on without you.

The Great Resignation

As of 2023, barely one in four workers worldwide feels engaged on the job—a Gallup record that also shows employee burnout scaling fresh heights.[2] These statistics say more about outdated systems than individual failings. COVID's harsh lessons stirred an awakening in most people—how we spend each fleeting Minute suddenly matters.

Seeking purpose, droves of people abandoned their burdensome jobs in 2022's "Great Resignation." Long treated as expendable assets, people suddenly wanted opportunities that recognized the importance of purpose-driven time. They wanted their Minutes to be spent meaningfully.

---

[2] Gallup. (2022). State of the Global Workplace: 2022 Report. Gallup Press. https://www.gallup.com/workplace/349484/state-of-the-global-workplace.aspx

The problem goes beyond any one company struggling to adapt. Even workers who won flexibility over their calendar still found it hard to engage. What many workers failed to realize during this time is that fulfilling lives require more than control—they require alignment across all areas. After all, what good is a flexible schedule if the work itself still fails to motivate?

Aligning Your Minutes with Your Purpose

True engagement depends on living a holistically energized life. But how do we build that? We build it one great decision at a time. No matter how hard the decision is. And therein lies the problem: it doesn't matter if we know what the best decision is for us if we still aren't willing to act on it.

Consider the case of Sarah, a marketing executive who found herself stuck in a job that no longer inspired her. She had a flexible schedule and a decent salary, but the work itself felt meaningless. She spent her days in meetings, discussing strategies that she knew would have little impact on the company's bottom line or the lives of its customers.

Sarah knew she needed a change, but the thought of leaving her comfortable job and starting over was daunting. She had bills to pay and a family to support. Plus, she wasn't even sure what kind of work would truly engage her.

One day, Sarah decided to take a hard look at how she was spending her Minutes. She realized that she was wasting hours each day on tasks that drained her energy and left her feeling unfulfilled. She knew that if she wanted to find true engagement, she would need to make some tough decisions.

Sarah started by setting aside time each week to explore her passions and interests. She took an online course in graphic design, something she had always been curious about but had never pursued. She volunteered at a local nonprofit, using her marketing skills to help them reach a wider audience. Slowly but surely, she began to rediscover the things that lit her up inside.

As Sarah gained clarity on what truly mattered to her, she began to make changes in her work life as well. She had honest conversations with her boss about her desire for more meaningful projects. She started to say no to meetings and tasks that didn't align with her values. And eventually, when an opportunity arose to join a mission-driven start-up, she took the leap.

Sarah's story illustrates the power of aligning our Minutes with our purpose. It's not always easy, and it often requires hard decisions and sacrifices. But when we invest our time in the things that truly matter to us, we open ourselves up to a world of possibility and fulfillment.

Practical Strategies for Maximizing Your Minutes

So, how can you start aligning your Minutes with your purpose? Here are a few practical strategies to try:

- Conduct a time audit: Keep a log of how you spend your time for a week, noting which activities leave you feeling energized and which ones drain you. Use this information to identify patterns and areas for improvement.
- Set clear priorities: Make a list of your top values and goals and use them as a filter for decision-making. Before saying yes to a new commitment, ask yourself whether it aligns with your priorities.

- Create space for exploration: Set aside regular time for activities that bring you joy and help you grow, whether it's learning a new skill, pursuing a hobby, or connecting with loved ones.
- Communicate your needs: If you're feeling disengaged at work, have an honest conversation with your boss or colleagues about what you need to feel more fulfilled. Be proactive in seeking out projects and roles that align with your strengths and interests.
- Embrace discomfort: Making changes in how you spend your time can be scary, but growth often lies on the other side of discomfort. Be willing to take calculated risks and step outside your comfort zone in pursuit of a more engaging life.

Make Minutes Matter

In a world that often values productivity over purpose, it's easy to let our Minutes slip away from us. But when we take charge of how we spend our time and align it with the things that truly matter to us, we open ourselves up to a life of engagement, fulfillment, and joy.

It's not always easy, and it requires hard work and tough decisions. But the alternative—a life of drift and disconnection—is no way to live. Your Minutes are precious. Spend them wisely.

So, what will you do with your next Minute?

CHAPTER 3

The Easy Road and the Hard Road

"Trust me, you don't want to be a teacher."

Like every high school student, I was required to meet with a guidance counselor before graduation. The goal of this meeting was to explore the many career options available at the time. With the help of an expert, I would be fully informed to choose my postgraduation path. A great idea, of course—except that I already knew what I was going to do with my life.

From the time I was small, I had my heart set on being a teacher. While the other kids were playing with their dolls at the park, I was lost in my own world, scribbling away on mini blackboards with chalk. When Christmas rolled around, Santa skipped the toys and instead stuffed my stocking with preschool workbooks and markers. I spent hours in the living room, corralling my siblings and cousins into makeshift classes, playing teacher until the sun went down. It was my calling, etched into my bones. I wanted to teach.

My family and friends were always in my corner. They knew I was born to teach. I was unshakable in my resolve and never second-guessed my path. But then, out of nowhere, my progress screeched to a halt as my high school counselor forced upon me a new reality. Suddenly I considered that perhaps there was another road I hadn't seen.

"No, that's not a good choice for you," the counselor said. "The field is flooded. Plus, you won't make any money that way. You're a smart girl with a good head on your shoulders. Teaching is just going to bore you. I don't think you'd be happy with that."

As I sat there, absorbing her words, a sense of confusion and doubt began to creep in. I had always been so sure of my path, but now I found myself questioning everything. Was she right? Would teaching really be a dead-end career for someone like me? The more I thought about it, the more I began to second-guess my long-held dreams.

What the counselor meant was, *It's a hard road to happiness, success, and fulfillment as a teacher. There is an easier road for someone like you.*

Her words struck me like a lightning bolt, jolting me out of my unwavering certainty. Prior to this, my universe was a harmonious chorus of support, where everyone rallied behind my every move. For the first time I was compelled to question the very foundation of my life's dream. How could I veer so far off course? Could she be the lone voice of reason, desperately trying to steer me away from a mistake that would forever alter my life? As the heavy burden of her words sank in, I realized that I couldn't ignore these nagging doubts.

"Well," I coughed out, trying to clear my suddenly thick throat, "if I don't teach, what would I do instead?"

The counselor squinted at me, then looked down at my paperwork, as if she were appraising a statue or some roadshow antique.

"Well, there are a lot of things you could do. I think you'd be a great lawyer, actually. Yes, you'd be a fabulous lawyer, Karen."

In that moment, the allure of a prestigious and well-paying career in law seemed to outweigh my lifelong passion for teaching. I found myself nodding along, convinced that this was the right path for me. The counselor's confidence in my abilities was flattering, and the prospect of financial stability was too tempting to resist.

In an instant, my world was turned upside down. I abandoned my lifelong aspirations to follow this new path. This decision, made quickly, would alter the trajectory of my life indefinitely.

My mom was familiar with my headstrong ways and knew that any opposition to my new plan would be fruitless. Though she was hesitant to see me give up my dream of being a teacher, both she and my father agreed to support my decision. This, to me, was further evidence I was making the right choice. They saw a law degree as admirable, and they wanted me to succeed.

The local university was the most financially viable option for my family. So, each day I took the grueling commute from my mother's house to the campus, my thoughts preoccupied with the new life that lay ahead. I was on the lawyer track. The "Easy Road."

Although I found some liberal arts subjects engaging, I had a nagging feeling I was neglecting my true passions. But with each passing semester, the idea of changing my path became more intimidating. I pushed forward, committed to seeing my journey through to the end. I raced through my undergrad years, grabbing my degree in a rush, and before I knew it I was deep in the prestigious world of law school. Four years gone, just like that.

To cover my law school expenses, I took a nine-to-five job. By day I worked in the city's corporate counsel's office, and by night I was a law school student. Every day I worked with lawyers, learned from lawyers, and went to school with people who wanted to be lawyers.

I hated every Minute of it.

Each day was a relentless tug-of-war between my head and my heart. My rational side insisted that I already invested too much time and money into this journey to turn back. It argued that abandoning the path would render all my efforts futile, and that the only sensible course of action was to press on and make peace with my choices.

Yet my heart refused to be ignored. My thoughts were constantly drawn back to my Christmas morning memories—a tiny, aspiring teacher patiently guiding her cousins through the art of coloring within the lines. No matter how many legal documents I pored over or how many pretrial conferences I attended, that little girl's silhouette stayed sharp in my thoughts.

As I struggled with this internal conflict, I began to realize the true cost of abandoning my passion. The long hours and grueling workload of law school left me feeling drained and unfulfilled. I longed for the sense of purpose and joy that I had once felt when imagining myself as a teacher. But still, I pressed on, convinced that I had come too far to turn back now.

It took me a full year of this to realize I had no interest in being a lawyer. Then, as the sun set on another grueling week, I hustled home from work, hastily swapped my bags, and then jetted off to a late Friday evening class. But amidst the chaos, I felt a sudden shift within me.

Epiphanies are often portrayed as jarring, like a slap in the face or a bucket of ice water dumped over one's head—a harsh awakening to reality. For me, however, this moment of clarity felt like a warm embrace, a comforting revelation that enveloped me as I stepped through the doorway of my mom's home. It was as if the universe itself had wrapped me in a gentle hug, providing shelter and validation for the thoughts that had been swirling in my mind. In that instant, I experienced a profound sense of certainty, a deep-seated knowledge that I had finally discovered my true path.

"I'm done," I said the next day at breakfast. "I'm not doing it anymore. It's terrible, I'm miserable, and I'm done."

My parents exchanged a look, communicating in a non-verbal language only shared by long-married couples. I saw flashes—fear, anger, compassion—but couldn't make out the entire unspoken conversation.

"Hmm. Okay, Karen, it's your life," my dad said finally, "but now you'd better go get yourself a job."

I did.

That weekend, I pored through the local newspaper's want ads (this was an age before home computers) and found a listing that proclaimed the opportunity to make over $500K per year—no experience required! Aha! On Monday, I called the hiring manager and he offered me the job over the phone.

As I hung up from the call, a sense of relief washed over me. I had finally taken a step toward reclaiming my life and pursuing a career that I believed would bring me fulfillment. However, in my haste to escape the world of law, I failed to consider whether this new path truly aligned with my passions and values.

Once more, my life careened off in a new direction, as unpredictable as a pinball bouncing from bumper to bumper. Gone were the days of legal pads and file folders; instead, I found myself making cold calls to sell capital equipment financing plans. It didn't take long for me to discover that this job was entirely commission-based, meaning my income was directly tied to my sales performance. If I couldn't close a deal, I wouldn't see a dime.

I initially believed this new plan would set me back on the right path, but it quickly became evident that I'd committed another serious blunder. I thought I was finally liberating myself to chase my true calling, but I discovered I'd inadvertently tied myself down even further. Yet again, I'd chosen the most convenient option—the Easy Road—that lay right before me instead of pausing to consider what would genuinely serve my long-term interests.

I was no closer to rediscovering my purpose.

The sales job was, incredibly, even more miserable than law school. I struggled through every sales pitch and spent a lot of time begging people to stop cursing at me. I couldn't close a single deal, which forced me to take out advances against my future earnings just to see a paycheck. For ten long months, I was "in the hole," borrowing against the promise of a potential sale that might never materialize.

As the weeks turned into months, I found myself sinking deeper into a state of despair. The constant rejection and financial strain took a heavy toll on my mental and emotional well-being. I felt trapped in a vicious cycle, unable to escape the consequences of my hasty decision.

A deep sense of dread consumed me. Getting out of bed each morning was a struggle. The ninety-minute commute to and from work only tired me further. I resented everyone around me—my coworkers, the people I talked to on the phone, and the bosses. Each day the job chipped away at my humanity. I felt trapped because the longer I stayed, the more debt

I accumulated, and the more hopeless my situation seemed. Whenever I tried to imagine a way out, all I saw was darkness.

For the first time in my life, I encountered what it truly meant to be disengaged. It wasn't just that my assignment was mind-numbingly dull—it was all-encompassing, devouring every Minute of my day and constantly demanding more. The hours I spent in the office left me utterly drained, and every moment I spent outside of work left me desperately trying to catch my breath and recover. I was perpetually exhausted.

I had to get out of the hole. I had to get out of the job. I had to get out. But I had no idea how.

As I reflected on my situation, I began to understand the root of my problem. By consistently choosing the Easy Road, I had strayed further and further from my true purpose. I had allowed external influences and short-term thinking to guide my decisions, rather than staying true to my authentic self.

At the time, I was unaware that my predicament was a direct result of choosing the Easy Road after high school rather than the Hard Road. Some might contend that a career in law is undoubtedly situated on the Hard Road, especially when compared with an education career. But the true difficulty of any path lies in how well it aligns with the person following it. In most cases, the Hard Road is the one that your heart yearns to follow—it's the adventure, the odyssey that calls out to the deepest parts of you. It's the one that puts everything on the line, but it's also the one with the most promising rewards.

The choice to take the Easy Road is one far too many people are prone to make, both at pivotal moments and in their day-to-day lives. The Easy Road is the path of least resistance—the obvious career choice, the nonconfrontational relationships, the fast-food meals five nights a week. It's the road that slowly numbs your sense of purpose until you're checked out, disengaged with life, and loaded with problems you lack motivation to solve.

The Hard Road is not without its own set of challenges, but when you choose a path that resonates with your sense of purpose, you will find that you are more eager to tackle the problems that arise. You'll be motivated to pore over lengthy fifty-page contracts, deliver persuasive sales pitches, and close deals with enthusiasm. You'll be driven to pursue the careers, relationships, and lifestyles that align with your authentic self, no matter the obstacles you encounter. You'll even fight to be financially stable, happy, liked, and fulfilled as a teacher!

Research has shown that individuals who pursue their true calling and align their actions with their values tend to experience greater job satisfaction, improved mental health, and a stronger sense of overall well-being.[3] A study by the *Harvard Business Review* found that employees who feel a sense of purpose in their work are more likely to be engaged, productive, and committed to their organizations.

Compared with the Easy Road, the Hard Road is undeniably more challenging. However, the Hard Road keeps you engaged, makes you feel more alive, and leads to greater fulfillment and success. And when we make decisions that keep us on this road, we'll find that we're happy with the way we spend our Minutes.

Still, most of us choose the Easy Road. I did, and I suffered the consequences. And no, I'm not just talking about a job I

---

3 "The Power of Purpose: How Companies Can Benefit from Fostering Meaningful Work," *Harvard Business Review*, accessed April 10, 2023, https://hbr.org/2018/11/the-power-of-purpose-how-companies-can-benefit-from-fostering-meaningful-work.

hated. You see, I ended up so disengaged with my life that I almost clocked out altogether.

The Force of a New Perspective

The initial step in freeing ourselves from wasting time in Bucket Three is acknowledging that we're doing it in the first place. Once we assess our situation, we can take action and make incremental progress to pull ourselves up and out. However, taking that first step is often the most challenging part of the process.

As a saleswoman, I knew my life wasn't brimming with promise, but I failed to recognize the extent of my desolation. It wasn't until my accident that I realized how far I had fallen.

It was a beautiful, sunny day in April, and I was late for work again. The traffic was horrendous thanks to ever-present road construction. I resigned myself to the inevitable reprimand I'd receive from the receptionist. True to form, the instant I arrived I was greeted by her accusatory tone.

"Nice of you to join us, Karen."

"Sure, yeah. I get it," I mumbled, trying to push past her to my desk. She stepped in front of me again, wearing a tight smile.

"There's someone who wants to speak with you," she said. "He's been calling all morning. I've run out of excuses for you. You'd better call him right now."

She thrust the stack of "While You Were Out" pink slips at me. I headed to my desk, found the right phone number, and called up this mystery man. A booming, jolly voice picked up the other end.

"Karen, good morning!" the voice bellowed. "I knew you'd turn up eventually. Today's your lucky day. I want to do some business with you!"

I recognized the voice. It was none other than my personal White Whale, a client I'd been pursuing for months. He was always courteous during our conversations, but we'd been playing an ongoing game of "cat and mouse." Each call ended with me sending him more and more information, seemingly moving further away from closing the deal. At least, that's what I thought. Once we moved past the initial pleasantries of the discussion, he agreed to move ahead with an $800,000 financing package.

The size of the deal baffled me. This would get me out of the hole, and then some, I thought. My head spun as he continued to talk.

"Just send me the paperwork and I'll get it all filled out when I can," he said.

No, I thought, *that's not good enough*. This sale would clear my debt with the company. I would actually make money for the first time in the job. I wasn't going to leave this deal up to a fax machine and a businessman's spare time.

"Oh, don't worry about that! Your office isn't far from mine," I lied. "I'll get the paperwork ready right now and deliver it to you in person!"

"That sounds fantastic, Karen. I'll see you soon," he said.

His office was a two-hour drive away. I collected the necessary paperwork as quickly as I could and hopped into my sporty 1979 Mercury Capri. As I flew down the highway, I felt as if I were in a dream. The entire conversation—the whole day—seemed so surreal that I half expected it to be a scam. I imagined arriving at the address only to find a decrepit building teeming with spiders and mice. However, when I reached my destination, there he was, waiting in the lobby with a check for his deposit.

When I left his office, the world felt different. It was about three o'clock in the afternoon as I climbed back into my car. The sun shone brilliantly, the breeze blew softly, and I was elated. I rolled down my windows and turned the radio up to its maximum volume. A thought crossed my mind: maybe, just maybe, I could turn my whole life around. Filled with a sense of triumph, I raised my hands toward the sky, letting the wind run through my fingers.

I didn't see the other car.

The impact was sudden and violent. The sickening crunch of metal against metal filled my ears as the world around me spun out of control. Pain exploded through my body as the dashboard crushed my chest, my ribs shattering under the immense force. My face slammed into the steering wheel, then bounced off the dash, before the windshield exploded, sending shards of glass flying in every direction.

It took paramedics two hours to cut me out of the mangled car. The dashboard was crushed into my chest, my ribs shattered. My face was a bloody, unrecognizable mess after smashing into the steering wheel, bouncing off the dash, and taking the worst of the windshield's explosion. The worst part—and the reason it took so long to free me from the wreck—was the emergency brake, which was buried about three inches deep in my right knee.

As the paramedics fought to keep me alive, I slipped in and out of consciousness. In the brief moments of lucidity, a storm of emotions swirled inside me, but embarrassment stood out above the rest. It wasn't the crash that made me cringe, but the naive optimism I'd felt just before it happened. How could I have been so stupid to think my life was about to change for the better? My existence was one big, cruel joke, and this accident was the ultimate punch line. I was a pathetic loser, a complete waste of space. What a mess my life had become.

Inside the ambulance, a paramedic radioed the hospital, urging them to contact my parents. They found their phone number in my purse. We were a good three hours from my parents' house—an agonizing journey for Mom and Dad to reach me. The ambulance arrived at the nearest hospital and medics rushed me into a room. A team of nurses hooked me up to a dizzying array of machines. As I watched the black screen flicker with green lines, my vital signs dancing chaotically, I realized that I might finally have a way out of my sorry existence.

"Karen?"

A nurse with kind eyes put a hand on my shoulder. "Be strong, Karen. You can pull through this. Your parents are on their way to see you."

"It…doesn't matter," I croaked, wincing a little. My whole body hurt. I was done with this world. It was time to move on to whatever was waiting for me on the other side.

The nurse saw right through my facade. "Of course it matters," she said. "You have to hold on. At least until your folks get here."

She sensed that I was hanging by a thread. Sure, my battered body was fighting tooth and nail to survive, but she looked beyond the physical wounds and straight into the emotional war raging inside me. She knew I was ready to let go, to slip away and leave this world behind. But she wasn't about to let me do that without a fight. With a gentle touch and a determined look in her eyes, she urged me to keep pushing, to hold on just a little longer.

"You have to let them say goodbye," she said, and I believed she was right. The least I could do was let my parents see me one last time.

The nurse sat with me during the hours it took my parents to arrive.

My father walked in, took one look at me, and fainted in a heap. This was a man who was tough as nails, but seeing his little girl so beat up was more than he could handle. Mom managed to stay on her feet, but the color drained from her face as she sank into one of the visitor's chairs, her legs no longer able to support her. The shock and pain etched on their faces was a gut-wrenching reflection of my terrible state.

They're here now, I thought. *I can finally let go.* And boy, was I tempted. I could feel the end, so close I could almost taste it. Every inch of me knew how easy it would be to just give in, to surrender to the darkness that beckoned me down. But as I watched my parents crumble at the sight of their little girl, broken and dying, I realized that my leaving would shatter them beyond repair. My choice to go—and I could feel it in my bones, it was a choice—would fracture something deep within them, leaving a gaping wound that would never heal.

I couldn't do that to them.

So, right then, I decided to stay.

And for the first time in my life, I chose the Hard Road.

The decision sent a ripple through my body, a small jolt of energy that brought me back to reality. I felt a little more awake, a little more present. Through hazy eyes, I watched the nurses help Dad off the floor, holding smelling salts under his nose. The doctor's voice cut through the chaos, informing him that they would need to amputate my right leg—the emergency brake was still lodged in my knee. Those words brought

Dad back to life, and he launched into a heated argument with the doctor. "You will not take her leg," he yelled, his voice raw with desperation. "Figure out another plan!" Mom, her face etched with worry, pulled her chair up beside me and rested a gentle hand on my bed, her touch reassuring both of us in different ways.

Before I knew it, a team of doctors whisked me away to surgery. Somehow, deep down, I had this unshakable feeling that I'd be back in the room with my parents soon. I wasn't ready to let go. I was determined to stick around, if not for myself, then for them.

In the days that followed, I gradually surfaced from a haze of trauma, exhaustion, and pain meds. The gravity of my situation settled heavily in my chest, like a lead weight threatening to drag me under. I came so close to death's door and I almost walked through it...willingly.

My life had veered so far off course, I had been ready to give up. Finding a way forward seemed too hard. There were too many obstacles in my way, too many demons to battle. It would have been easier to surrender, to let go. Especially now that I was staring down the prospect of a long, grueling recovery.

During my hospital stay, my parents kept vigil in those uncomfortable visitor's chairs. Sometimes my siblings were there too, their presence a comforting reminder that I wasn't alone. One day, I noticed a teddy bear and some flowers on the table beside my bed, a small gesture of love and support. As I looked at my family, I realized they seemed so much like that teddy bear from my perspective: small, fragile, and infinitely precious. It was a poignant reminder of why I chose the path of recovery, why I decided to fight my way back to them.

Work never crossed my mind. I didn't waste a single moment worrying about how my injuries would impact my ability to hold a job or be productive at the office. If anything, I felt oddly grateful for the awful circumstances that prevented me from going back. It wasn't until much later that I had a startling realization: my job simply wasn't worth the time, effort, or emotional anguish I poured into it. I would have rather died.

Getting Back on the Road

Okay, Karen, I told myself, *if you're going to stick around, you're going to have to figure out how to make it worth the effort.* This, of course, was easier to think about than to do, especially from a hospital bed.

In the months following the accident, three significant challenges shaped my recovery process. The first was a substantial amount of internal bleeding that the doctors overlooked until my second day in the hospital. My unstable condition required the medical team's constant attention.

The second issue was the state of my leg. While the doctors agreed to save it, they were convinced that I would never regain the ability to walk. My dad, however, refused to accept this prognosis. With a firm but encouraging tone, he reassured me that if I wanted to keep my leg for the rest of my life, I would need to find a way to use it again, proving the doctors wrong.

The third challenge was perhaps the most unsettling: I was not allowed to see my face. The doctors were worried that if I caught a glimpse of my appearance, it would send me into a state of shock. Everyone around me took great care to remove any reflective surfaces from my room, and even though I was confined to the bed, someone covered the bathroom mirror with a spare blanket. This unknown aspect terrified me the most—just how bad could my face look? My imagination ran wild, conjuring up images of a grotesque, disfigured monster staring back at me.

As I lay there, contemplating the long road ahead, I realized that my recovery would be about more than just healing my physical wounds. It would be a journey of self-discovery, a chance to reconnect with my true purpose and find the courage to pursue it, no matter how difficult the path may be.

I knew that I couldn't go back to my old life, to the disengagement and dissatisfaction that had nearly cost me everything. I had to find a new way forward, one that aligned with my authentic self and gave me a reason to keep fighting.

With this newfound determination, I threw myself into the recovery process. I worked tirelessly with physical therapists to regain strength and mobility in my leg, pushing through the pain and frustration with gritted teeth and a stubborn refusal to give up. I also began to explore my inner world, reflecting on my past choices and the values that truly mattered to me.

As the weeks turned into months, I made slow but steady progress. The doctors marveled at my resilience, and my family's unwavering support gave me the strength to keep going. And as I healed, both physically and emotionally, I began to see a glimmer of hope on the horizon—a future where I could pursue my true calling and live a life of purpose and fulfillment.

The accident was a turning point, a brutal wake-up call that forced me to confront the reality of my life. It was a reminder that time is precious and that every moment we spend disengaged or unfulfilled is a moment wasted. The Easy Road had led me to a dead end, and it was time to chart a new course.

As I prepared to leave the hospital and embark on the next phase of my journey, I made a promise to myself: I would never again settle for a life that didn't align with my true purpose. I would embrace the Hard Road, no matter how challenging it may be, because I knew that it was the only path to genuine happiness and success.

Looking back, I realize that the accident was a blessing in disguise. It shattered the illusions that had held me back and forced me to confront the truth about my life. It gave me the courage to pursue my dreams and the clarity to see what truly mattered.

Today, as I navigate the twists and turns of the Hard Road, I am grateful for the lessons I learned and the strength I gained from that harrowing experience. I now know that the journey ahead will be difficult, but I am ready to face whatever challenges come my way. Because now, I am living a life that is true to myself—a life of purpose, passion, and endless possibility.

The Force of a New Perspective

The initial step in freeing ourselves from wasting time in Bucket Three is acknowledging that we're doing it in the first place. Once we assess our situation, we can take action and make incremental progress to pull ourselves up and out. However, taking that first step is often the most challenging part of the process.

As a saleswoman, I knew my life wasn't brimming with promise, but I failed to recognize the extent of my desolation. It wasn't until my accident that I realized how far I had fallen. The crash was a brutal wake-up call, a jarring reminder of the consequences of my choices. It forced me to confront the reality of my disengagement and the toll it had taken on my life.

But it also gave me a new perspective, a clarity of purpose that I had never experienced before. As I lay in that hospital bed, fighting for my life, I realized that I had been given a second chance—an opportunity to start over and create a life that truly mattered.

That realization was the driving force behind my recovery and the catalyst for the changes I would make in the years to come. It gave me the courage to pursue my true calling, even when the path was difficult and the obstacles seemed insurmountable.

Looking back, I can see that the accident was a turning point, a defining moment that altered the course of my life. It was the wake-up call I needed to break free from the Easy Road and embrace the Hard Road, the path of purpose and fulfillment.

And as I continue on this journey, I am reminded every day of the power of perspective. When we change the way we see the world, we change the way we live in it. We find the courage to pursue our dreams, the strength to overcome our challenges, and the wisdom to make choices that align with our true selves.

So if you find yourself stuck in Bucket Three, wasting your Minutes on things that don't matter, I encourage you to take a step back and examine your life from a new perspective. Ask yourself what truly matters to you, what gives your life meaning and purpose. And then, have the courage to pursue it, no matter how difficult the path may be.

Because in the end, the Hard Road is the only road worth taking. It's the road that leads to a life of passion, purpose, and endless possibility. And it all starts with a single step, a decision to break free from the Easy Road and embrace the journey ahead.

Take that step today. Your future self will thank you for it.

CHAPTER 4

The Line Between Job and Purpose

A Three Bucket Leader recognizes that for every person there is a job, and there is a purpose, and those two factors don't have to align perfectly to live a fulfilling life. This is true for leaders, followers, and the people somewhere in between. The key to valuable Minutes lies in the balance between job and purpose.

After a grueling eighteen-month recovery from my accident, I set out on a journey to find the right job—a role that would align with my values, passions, and aspirations. Although I didn't have a name for it yet, I knew I'd spent far too long languishing in what I would later call "Bucket Three." This time around, I was determined not to settle for a job that would consume all my precious time and energy. I refused to be trapped in a vicious cycle of unfulfilling work that drained my spirit and robbed me of satisfaction. I wanted a professional path that would allow me to do more than survive—I wanted to thrive.

With limited resources at my disposal, I relied on my mother to drive me through Chicago's bustling streets for all my job interviews. I engaged with executives, hiring managers, and HR teams from numerous companies. Some declined to move forward, but plenty of them had something to offer.

"We want you to come on and join our marketing team."

"You'd be an incredible addition to our product team."

"We think you'd be a great fit for our finance department."

They were good offers. Some of them were great offers. But I turned them all down with a soft smile, saying, "It sounds like an amazing opportunity, but it's not for me."

After fourteen months I had burned through nearly every recruiter in the greater Chicago area. In fact, I'd earned myself a nice reputation among recruiting teams. I was "that woman no one in Chicagoland can place."

"You've got to tell me what you want, Karen," one recruiter said after I rejected her for the third time.

"I don't know what I want," I said honestly, "but I'll know it when I find it."

While I waited for my career to reveal itself, I still needed money. I had bills to pay, and although I'd never admit it openly, I needed to get out of my parents' house. After eighteen months of bed rest in a room less than thirty feet from Mom and Dad's fussing, I couldn't even walk to the bathroom without hearing, "Karen? Are you okay? Do you need help?" It was all out of love, of course, but a young woman needs some privacy.

With the last of my savings from my sales job, I moved to a vibrant apartment on Chicago's North Side. I was surrounded by young professionals, a thrilling nightlife, and an electrifying atmosphere. The area's excellent public transportation granted me the freedom to move around the city with ease, which allowed me to expand my job search without relying on my mother's assistance. However, time was of the essence—I had thirty days to secure enough income for rent and only five days before my food supply ran out.

On my first night in the new apartment, I carefully reviewed my résumé, searching for signs of untapped potential or connections I hadn't considered before. Despite my strong aversion to sales positions, I couldn't deny my talent in this area...provided I had face-to-face interactions with clients.

Sales let me exercise my teaching abilities. Selling a product was simply a matter of educating the customer and providing them with the information they needed to make an informed decision. I realized I could return to a sales role, so long as it didn't cost my integrity.

As I continued my job search, I found solace in my daily walks through the city, which not only helped my recovering leg but also cleared my mind. It was during one of these walks that I stumbled upon Bigsby & Kruthers, a high-end men's clothing store that seemed to call out to me. Little did I know that this chance encounter would lead me to a transformative experience.

After several days of deliberation, I decided to take action. Dressed in my most professional attire, I strode through the doors of Bigsby & Kruthers. As I crossed the threshold, I was immediately enveloped by the rich aroma of fine leathers, sophisticated colognes, and meticulously polished woods. The soft lighting cast a warm glow on the displays of exquisite suits and accessories, each piece carefully arranged to entice the discerning customer. The faint sound of classical music mingled with the hushed conversations of the sales associates and their clients, creating an atmosphere of refined luxury.

I found the assistant manager helping a customer. When he finished, I approached him with a big smile and said, "I'd like to sell clothes here."

He snickered at me. "I'm sorry, my dear. Perhaps you didn't notice, but this is a men's clothing store. We only hire male sales associates."

Undeterred, I raised my eyebrow and plainly ignored his rejection. "I'm telling you, sir, if you bring me on, you won't regret it. I can do this job—and I will make your customers happy while earning us both a lot of money."

I handed him a copy of my résumé and a personalized cover letter. He skimmed both, occasionally nodding at the words on the pages. Then he looked me up and down—a young five-foot-nothing lady with a slight limp and a sharp, tenacious personality.

He must have seen something he liked, because after a moment he said, "You know what? You might be right. I bet you could do us some good. Are you free to start next Monday?"

While Bigsby & Kruthers wasn't the dream job I had in mind, it turned out to be an incredible opportunity. This high-end store was the go-to place for Chicago's elite, including star athletes from the Bulls and Bears. I formed strong bonds with everyone at the store, from the cashiers to my fellow salesmen, creating a real sense of teamwork and camaraderie. My commissions were impressive—the merchandise often carried price tags higher than my monthly rent. As the only female in a men's clothing store, my perspective was highly valued by customers, who often wanted a woman's opinion on their fashion choices.

I was engaged with my work, which left me with the time, energy, and drive I needed to continue my career search.

My life fell into a comfortable routine. From Wednesday to Saturday, I spent my mornings attending job interviews, then shifted gears to work at Bigsby during the afternoons and evenings. On Sundays, Mom picked me up and brought me home to spend my days off with the family. We enjoyed cozy dinners together, and I pitched in around the house whenever I could.

My dad, who had never shown much enthusiasm for my previous jobs, took a keen interest in my work at Bigsby, eagerly asking about my experiences and responsibilities. It was a welcome change, and I started looking forward to our conversations, sharing the highlights of my week and the interesting characters I encountered at the store.

"How much did you sell this week?" he'd ask. I'd give him a number and he'd laugh in disbelief. Every once in a while I'd regale him with stories about Michael Jordan's newest suit or the sweater Mike Ditka bought from me earlier in the week.

On Tuesdays, I'd head back to my apartment, ready to jump back into my routine at Bigsby and continue my job hunt. I never dreaded the return.

I worked the same amount of Minutes as I did in law school. In fact, my schedule was even more packed, but I was fully engaged with my new work. Each day brought new excitement about the possibilities ahead, even when I declined job offers that didn't quite fit my aspirations. The path before me shone brighter than ever, even without a clear destination in sight.

A Job, a Purpose, and Work

My time at Bigsby & Kruthers was more than just a temporary job; it was a period of personal growth and discovery. As I immersed myself in the world of high-end fashion and forged meaningful connections with my colleagues and customers, I began to reflect on the deeper meanings of job, purpose, and work. This period of my life, though transitional, was filled with some of the most engaging moments I'd ever experienced. I wasn't a teacher, and I didn't yet know how much my life would change, but none of it mattered. I was living in the present, fully engaged in what I now recognize as Bucket One—feeling truly alive and making the most of every Minute.

The experiences at the store taught me valuable lessons about the difference between a job, a purpose, and work. A job gives you an employee status, a set of responsibilities, and a paycheck...but it doesn't necessarily give you a purpose. A job is a means to an end—whether that's money, fulfillment, or some much-needed time out of the house. When I worked at McDonald's in high school, it was just a job. Selling capital equipment financing before my accident was definitely just a job. Working at Bigsby was also a job, but sometimes jobs are exciting and fun. Other times, they're a means to an end— nothing more than a prerequisite to affording to spend your weekends the way you want.

These valuable lessons would shape my understanding of what it means to live a fulfilling life, and they would guide me in my pursuit of a career that aligned with my true purpose.

Work, to me, is an expression of who you are. Engaged work is joyous, while disengaged work is a slog. When you're young, work is play. Then, work becomes schoolwork, homework, and housework. Later in life, work may be between the hours of nine to five, but it's also when you make dinner, tidy up, and read before bed.

When you're old, work is how you choose to spend your retirement. The work you do every day might not always align with your calling, but the effort you put in still matters. Every task, no matter how small, takes work. How you decide to put in work shapes your character, builds your skills, and guides you toward your purpose. If you engage with your work, it will energize you. If you don't engage, it will drain you.

Purpose is another matter. Asking, "What is purpose?" is like asking, "What's the meaning of life?" We could dive deep into philosophy, psychology, maybe even biology here, but I want to keep it simple. So, here's my definition: your purpose is what guides you, motivates you, and feels the most fulfilling when you're engaged with it. The Minutes you spend in Bucket One are the ones you spend aligned with your purpose. However, these Minutes don't have to be spent on your job. Sometimes you work a job to free up time to work toward your purpose.

For example, if your purpose is to be an entrepreneur, you may need to build your bank account before venturing off on your own. The Minutes you spend working at a local grocery store, restaurant, or gas station still contribute to your purpose. You're investing in your future. After work, the Minutes you spend taking classes, networking with business owners, and watching *Shark Tank* also contribute to your purpose.

When you know your purpose, you know how to tell the difference between the Easy Road and the Hard Road. You know the difference between an hour of watching TV versus an hour spent writing that novel stuck in your head. You know the difference between sleeping in versus getting up and clearing your head with a workout or meditation. You know how to make a great decision, one that puts your Minutes into Bucket One.

This just leaves one missing piece to the puzzle: What is your purpose?

What Makes You Tick?

For many, the task of pinpointing their purpose feels daunting. Even those who already know their purpose may struggle to find a job that perfectly aligns with it. The real challenge for most isn't a lack of purpose but rather a lack of clarity on what it is.

Finding your purpose starts with a simple question: "What makes me come alive?" It's not too hard to ask the question and journal a few answers, but you must take the time to ask and answer. When you dig deep and identify what inspires you, you're well on your way to uncovering your true calling.

While your dream job might not be within reach just yet, there are ways to make this waiting period count. During my own waiting phase, I worked at Bigsby & Kruthers. I didn't waste Minutes there; I invested them, saving them up for the moment the perfect job appeared.

Then, about a year into my job at Bigsby, I came home one Friday evening to a blinking light on my answering machine. (For those who don't know, this device preceded the convenience of voicemail.) The machine had three messages for me.

The first: "Hi, my name is Scott and I'm a recruiter. Give me a call."

The second, recorded one hour later: "Hi, it's Scott again, the recruiter. I'm leaving a message for the elusive woman in Chicagoland that no recruiter can place. I've got a position for her, so she'd better call me back, fast."

The third, only an hour after the second: "Karen, listen, I need you to call me back tomorrow. I know it's Saturday, but this is important. I've got your dream job."

Hmm, I thought, *what's with this guy?*

By this point, most recruiters had given up on me. I hadn't heard of Scott, but I had copies of my résumé floating all around the city at this point. I decided to give him a call the next morning. Even if I wasn't particularly interested in what he had to say, I figured that reaching out would at least prevent him from further cluttering the audiotape on the answering machine.

"Karen!" he answered right away. "You called! What took you so long?"

I laughed. "It's been eight hours, Scott. I was busy!"

"Well, lucky you. Anyway, I think I'm going to achieve the impossible here. I think I've got the job for you. Interested?"

"Sure," I said.

"All right, so here's the scoop—it's not a sales job. There are no heavy quotas, so let's clear the air on that from the start. I'm working with a big bank, and I can't reveal which one just yet, but they've recently launched a brand-new product. It's a pretty big deal—completely new to the market, but the catch is that customers need some training before they can start using it. That's where you come in—you'd be the person to step in and educate these customers once they've purchased the product. But that's not all! The bank also needs you to keep an eye on these relationships, just to ensure that everything's running smoothly. So, in essence, no sales pressure, just focusing on building and maintaining solid customer relationships. Are you interested?"

"I am," I said, and I meant it. I felt an energy well up inside me at the sound of this job. I felt an incredible tug toward the unknown, the same one I felt for Bigsby, but ten times stronger.

"Great. I'm scheduling you for an interview on Monday morning at 8:30 a.m. The recruiting team is flying in over the weekend, and they want to start talking with candidates first thing."

He gave me the details and wished me good luck. I thanked him for the call, hung up, and started interview prep that day. By Monday, I had a fresh new stack of résumés, a perfectly rehearsed set of interview responses, and a sharp interview outfit. I was buzzing with excitement.

When I arrived on Monday morning, I was shocked to see over forty other people in the waiting area. *What are they doing here?* I thought. *This is my job! Why are they wasting their time?* I sat glaring at the competition for half an hour. Finally, a receptionist stood at the front of the tiny waiting room and explained the process to the growing crowd of candidates. We learned that we'd meet with two people. The first interview would be short—fifteen, maybe twenty minutes with a senior executive from the bank. The second discussion would be a bit longer, and this one would be with the hiring manager.

I waited for three agonizing hours before the receptionist finally called my name. That's when I stepped into the first conference room and encountered Patricia, right in the midst of her lunch. She was a tall, slender woman, and I couldn't help but notice her expensive attire. I wondered if her ego would match the pocketbook that afforded her such fancy clothes.

As Patricia motioned for me to take a seat at the table, a tomato slice escaped from her sandwich, sending a spray of mayonnaise across her papers. It was at that moment that I caught a glimpse of her striking blue eyes, which crinkled with laughter as she surveyed the mess. While we worked together to clean up the unexpected catastrophe, Patricia and I clicked instantly. We dove into a lively conversation that lasted for over an hour, our rapport growing stronger by the minute. Just as we were fully immersed in our discussion, we were interrupted by a sudden banging on the doors.

"We have to keep moving," a voice said from the other side.

Patricia gave me an apologetic smile and said, "Oh, I'm sorry about that. It's been so lovely chatting with you. I wish we had more time."

"It has been fun. I feel like we're already friends," I said. "How long are you in town? Do you have time to meet tomorrow for a coffee?"

"Oh, that would be fun, but I'm afraid we're shipping off to Pittsburgh later tonight. This position is part of a national team, and the mid-Atlantic position is next up for interviews."

"Well, maybe I can help you close the loop on the Chicago opening! Do I have the job?" I said.

She laughed. "You've got my vote, that's for sure. But now you'll need to talk with Dawn. If you ever find yourself in New York, give me a call. Here's my card."

As I walked through the next set of doors, I discovered to my dismay that Dawn was Patricia's antithesis. She sat rigidly behind her desk, her lips pressed into a thin line, and her eyes narrowed as she appraised me. Her short, clipped responses to my greeting set the tone for the rest of the interview. As she described the job, her monotonous voice and dismissive demeanor made it clear that she saw me as just another candidate, not as a potential asset to the team.

Despite her cold reception, I refused to be deterred. I listened intently to her description of the role, asking thoughtful questions and highlighting my relevant skills and experiences. I maintained a confident and enthusiastic tone, determined to prove that I was the perfect fit for the position, regardless of Dawn's apparent indifference.

As the interview drew to a close, Dawn's expression softened slightly. She leaned back in her chair and said, "Well, Karen, I must admit that you're not what I expected. You seem to have a good grasp of the position and a genuine passion for the work. We'll be in touch."

I left the interview feeling a mix of emotions. While my conversation with Patricia had been incredibly positive, my interaction with Dawn left me uncertain about my chances. Nevertheless, I remained hopeful, knowing that I had done my best to showcase my abilities and enthusiasm for the role.

The week following my interviews was filled with a mixture of anticipation and nervousness. Each day seemed to drag on endlessly as I waited for news about the job. I found myself constantly checking my phone messages, hoping for a call from Scott or Patricia. At night, I lay awake, replaying every moment of the interviews in my mind, analyzing each word and gesture, trying to gauge my chances of landing the position.

As the days passed, my excitement grew. I started to envision myself in the role, imagining the challenges I would face and the successes I would achieve. I became increasingly confident that I would receive good news, and I even started making tentative plans for my future in the new job.

However, when I called Scott the following Monday for an update, my hopes were shattered. Instead of the job offer I had been expecting, I learned that the position was awarded to an internal candidate—a friend of Dawn's who wanted to relocate from Atlanta to Chicago. The news hit me like a punch to the gut, leaving me feeling deflated and confused.

The rejection was crushing. I didn't understand how this job, this perfect spot for me, slipped through my fingers. From the moment I heard about it, I couldn't imagine doing anything else. And now it was gone.

Except…it wasn't, was it?

The Easy Road would have been to accept my fate quietly and submit to the growing chip on my shoulder. To let frustration wash me back to the dark days before my accident. To accept the consolations of my family and friends and go back to selling men's suits, waiting for the next opportunity to come along. But I didn't want another opportunity. I wanted this one.

I hung up with Scott and sat alone in my mom's kitchen. I'd spent the weekend telling my family about the job and the incredible journey I was about to undertake. I couldn't bear the idea of staying an extra day dealing with everyone's well-meaning consolations for my bad luck. I wanted to go back to my apartment.

Mom and I piled into the car and set out for Chicago's North Side. As I sulked in silence, my mind played through every detail of both interviews on repeat. My thoughts searched for the moment where I went wrong. Instead, I remembered something different. What was it that Patricia said about the job being part of a national team?

"Mom, can you pull over up there?" I pointed at a Dunkin' Donuts off the side of the highway. She barely put the car in park before I barreled out toward a nearby pay phone. (We're still in the era before cell phones.) Pulling Patricia's business card out of my purse, I punched in the telephone number at the bottom and waited.

"Hello, this is Pat."

"Pat!" I said. "It's Karen, the candidate from Chicago. I just heard I didn't get the job."

"Oh, Karen, yes, I'm so sorry about that. It was close, and I fought hard for you. But ultimately, an internal candidate unexpectedly raised her hand and we needed to give the job to her. You were such a great candidate, though, and I'll definitely keep in touch. You never know, things can change! Maybe next time—"

"Pat," I interrupted, "how did things go in Pittsburgh?"

"Actually, it was a waste of time. We didn't see the same caliber of candidates out there. We're headed back for another round of interviews next week," she said.

"No need," I said. "I'll take it."

"What do you mean?"

"The Pittsburgh job. I'll take it."

She paused.

"You want the Pittsburgh position? Are you sure, Karen? You'd have to move...and move fast...I'm not sure we can make it happen."

"We can make it happen. I'll move faster than you've ever seen anyone move. I'm sure. I want that job. Call who you need to call, make whatever arrangements you need, and let me know when to pack up. I know this is a good decision. For both of us."

Pat sighed a little, but it quickly grew into a laugh. I could practically see those sparkling blue eyes crinkling with joy again. "All right, Karen. Let's get to work."

The Road Ahead

Making the decision to take the Pittsburgh job was a turning point in my life. It was a bold move, one that required me to step out of my comfort zone and embrace the unknown. But I knew in my heart that it was the right choice, a choice that aligned with my purpose and my desire to make a meaningful impact. As I hung up the phone with Patricia, I felt a surge of excitement and determination. I was ready to embark on this new chapter, to face the challenges and opportunities that lay ahead.

As I settled into my new role, I found that the job was everything I had hoped for and more. I thrived on the opportunity to educate customers and build meaningful relationships, using my skills and passion to make a real difference in people's lives. And while the work was demanding, I approached each day with a sense of purpose and engagement, knowing that I was exactly where I was meant to be.

Looking back on this experience, I realize that finding a balance between job and purpose is a journey that requires introspection, perseverance, and a willingness to take risks. It's not always easy, and there may be setbacks and detours along the way. But by staying true to ourselves and pursuing work that aligns with our values and passions, we can make the most of every Minute and live a truly fulfilling life.

My own journey taught me that when we dare to follow our hearts and take bold steps toward our dreams, incredible things can happen. By embracing the unknown and trusting in ourselves, we open the door to a world of possibilities and opportunities for growth, both personally and professionally.

So, as you navigate your own journey, remember to ask yourself: "What makes me come alive?" Seek out opportunities that align with your values and passions, and don't be afraid to take risks in pursuit of your dreams. By doing so, you'll find that the Minutes you spend engaged in work that matters will compound over time, leading you to a life of purpose, satisfaction, and true success.

PART TWO

Reengaging for
a Better Life

CHAPTER 5

Capital-M Minutes

Landing my dream job as an account manager was a pivotal moment in my career, but it came with a startling realization: my personal work ethic alone wouldn't suffice to make me a valuable team member. As the new person, I had to tune into my team's rhythms and recognize that their time was as precious as my own.

Adapting to my new role required mastering unfamiliar tasks such as strategic scheduling, progress tracking, and workload balancing. The grueling job search had built my resolve, but connecting with colleagues demanded patience and understanding. My dream job wasn't just about me—it was about enabling an entire team to invest their Minutes with purpose and impact, creating a shared rhythm that pulsed with the heartbeat of meaningful work.

The first few months were a whirlwind of change and excitement. I packed up my life and moved into a tiny, barebones apartment in Pittsburgh, but the job required so much traveling that I hardly spent any time there. In fact, for the first year of the job, I lived mostly in Buffalo, New York, near the operations center for our new product.

To effectively help customers understand the product, the company believed I needed to understand it inside and out first. I spent a month embedded in each of the twelve departments working on it, learning every aspect of the product. One year later, I emerged as an expert, my mind brimming with knowledge and my heart full of pride.

I loved every Minute of that year.

The travel, client-needs assessments, and collaborations with dozens of functional teams—I soaked it all up. Before this job, I'd never traveled farther than a few hours outside of Chicago. Suddenly, I was zipping from Buffalo to California and then back to New York. Almost every Minute felt more engaging than the last. I was finally All In.

For the first time in my life, my Minutes were landing solely in Bucket One. My work felt like the best use of my time and talents. However, one obstacle threatened my Bucket One existence: Dawn, my manager.

A chill ran down my spine the moment I saw her on my first day, her pursed lips and narrowed eyes sending a clear message of disapproval. I didn't blame her for the icy glare—I'm sure I would have felt slighted too. But her obvious disdain threatened this new chapter of my life. Despite our bumpy history, I reminded myself that we were now colleagues with a chance to start fresh. I was determined to prove I was more than a manipulative job-hopper.

As the months unfolded, I resolved to thaw the chill between us. I asked for her advice, complimented her leadership, and worked harder than anyone on our team. My goal wasn't just to earn her approval but to gain her respect through dedication and teamwork. If I could win over someone as skeptical as her, I knew I could succeed in this new role.

It was not to be.

Our working relationship was a constant tug-of-war, a clash of opposing forces that threatened to implode with every encounter. I was a blazing comet, streaking through each day with fiery enthusiasm. She, on the other hand, was a steady anchor, a cool and measured presence focused on maintaining stability and consistency. While I aimed to inspire bold, new thinking, she valued the comforting efficiency of the well-trodden path.

Dawn's discomfort with her job was evident in her half-hearted interactions and checked-out attitude, and it bothered me more than anything else about her. She may have been great at managing things, but she wasn't a great fit for managing people. And this led to some serious leadership problems.

Dawn created an environment that discouraged engagement, making interacting with her difficult for the team. Most of my colleagues followed her orders to avoid attracting her ire, and few felt the freedom needed to engage customers in the ways they wanted.

Though our intentions were pure, our differing temperaments bred frequent tension and misunderstandings. We were two forces of nature, destined to collide. Perhaps, given time and effort, we might have found a way to harness our contrasting energies, but the friction between us too often obscured the light.

Dawn was only three years older than me, and this was her first management job. On paper, she wasn't any more qualified than the rest of us, but she was put in charge. We were all new to the job, learning as we went, but Dawn had the authority.

Some days, frustration bubbled inside me as I witnessed Dawn's management style. I felt like I was learning faster and making better decisions. I cared more about the work and the people who supported the customers. Why was she the one managing me when I seemed better suited for it?

Dawn's disengaged, militaristic style drained the team's creativity and made enjoying work impossible for many. But not me. While her miserable management demoralized others, it lit a fire within me. As she suppressed creativity with an iron fist, it fueled my determination to prove a flexible approach worked better.

I realized Dawn wasn't just disengaged with me, she was disengaged with everyone and everything. She wasted her Minutes on the job, and her frustration trickled down to her employees.

This toxic dynamic lasted three painful years. In the third year, everything changed for Dawn. She married, became pregnant, and stepped down from her management role. Once unshackled from a job she never meshed with, she finally found true fulfillment in the prospect of motherhood.

For those of us who suffered under her management, watching Dawn preparing to become a mom was both bewildering and vindicating. And as Dawn handed off responsibilities and readied for her baby, a collective sigh of relief rippled through the office, the tension dissipating like a heavy fog lifting at last.

It was time to replace Dawn.

Unfortunately, management's efforts to revive our demoralized team proved misguided. Dawn was replaced by Robert—her hand-picked successor—which didn't leave room for real change. Like Dawn, Robert understood little about cultivating an innovative, customer-centric environment.

Robert seemed more engaged than Dawn at first but soon encountered a common challenge for first-time managers:

effectively coaching others on time management. Instead of providing guidance on solving customer issues, Robert spent considerable time counseling the team on personal matters.

Robert's interpersonal skills were so underdeveloped that he couldn't figure out what the team needed to meet rising expectations. His failure to connect personally with team members and customers crippled his leadership efforts.

Frustrated by this shortcoming, Robert shifted from gently guiding the team to barking orders. His forced "people-centric" approach only highlighted his discomfort and lack of self-awareness in leading the team. He placed excessive importance on specific behaviors and body language, hoping they would project the desired image. However, this forced approach backfired, further hindering his ability to build genuine connections.

Robert's leadership deficiencies quickly caught the attention of senior management. In an attempt to salvage the situation, the division manager stepped in and advised Robert to plan a team-building exercise as a way to redeem himself in the eyes of his group and upper management. To ensure a successful and impactful event, a generous budget was allocated.

However, Robert's frugal mindset, a result of his upbringing in a large family, drove him to make the misguided decision to charter a boat for the team-building activity without arranging for any food or beverages. It was a choice that fell far short of expectations.

On the day of the retreat, our team arrived at the port, the scorching sun beating down on our backs as we lugged heavy bags of groceries, the heat sapping our energy and souring our moods. It was ninety-eight humid degrees, and we were miserable.

Huddled on the end of the dock, we waited for Robert to tell us which boat to board, but he didn't know. Renee, a team member, took charge and found the boat information, highlighting Robert's lack of preparation. Pulling a paper from her bag, she proclaimed Row J/Slip 22 to be our destination.

We all scuffled down to the center of Row J, only to find that the slips were poorly marked. Robert agonized over the decision of which direction to go. Frustrated by the situation, I decided to investigate the left side, the wooden planks creaking beneath my determined steps. Interestingly, when I started walking, the entire team followed me.

We reached the end of Row J, the air thick with disappointment as we realized we'd walked in the wrong direction. Everyone groaned, and Robert blamed me for leading us the wrong way.

As the group shuffled back toward the right end of Row J, Robert hung back to talk to me. "You don't understand," he said, his voice tinged with a mix of admiration and envy. "People follow you, Karen. You don't have to ask. They just do—and that's a big responsibility. I wish they'd do that for me."

Robert's words echoed in my mind, their weight settling on my shoulders. I had emerged as the leader of the group, even without a formal managerial role. It dawned on me then—a realization that so many managers, including Robert, fail to grasp when they step into leadership roles: if I was responsible for managing how others worked, I also had a responsibility to make the time they worked worthwhile.

My frustration at the dock led to a critical leadership mistake—I failed to communicate my intent to the team, unintentionally wasting their Minutes. However, this misstep inadvertently showcased my leadership potential. Despite lacking a formal title, I took charge and guided the team. Robert recognized it right away, and it ultimately paved the way for more official leadership roles later in my career.

This experience taught me an invaluable lesson: valuing others' time and using it effectively is paramount for a leader. Leaders often assume others will understand their desired outcome without explicitly stating it, resulting in misused time and effort as people act on assumptions rather than clear direction. Wandering aimlessly and wasting company time is the hallmark of immature leadership. Top-of-the-line leaders, on the other hand, communicate clearly, provide explicit direction, and ensure every Minute is utilized productively toward stated goals.

As I advanced into positions with greater responsibility, this lesson served me well. Effective leadership demands clear communication, alignment of understanding, and a relentless focus on making every Minute worthwhile. However, to manage others' Minutes effectively, I needed an effective way of talking about Minutes. This is where the concept of "Buckets" came into play.

Buckets of Minutes: A Framework for Effective Time Management

Every Minute of our lives is precious, and how we choose to invest those Minutes determines their value and impact. At the end of every sixty seconds, that Minute is irrevocably allocated into one of three buckets:

- Bucket One: Minutes invested in activities that enrich your life, advance your goals, and create lasting value.

- Bucket Two: The "Limbo Bucket," where decisions are suspended, disengagement exists, and time is spent without meaningful impact.
- Bucket Three: Minutes spent in despair, seemingly trapped in negative situations. People here have lost hope, but this deep anguish can trigger a radical awakening that begins the challenging journey toward positive change.

The key to a fulfilling and impactful life lies in consciously directing your Minutes into Bucket One as often as possible, minimizing the Minutes that leak into Bucket Two, and avoiding the poisonous pit of Bucket Three at all costs. With disciplined time investment into enriching activities, your Minutes compound into a legacy of achievement, growth, and well-being.

The "Bucket Journal" is a powerful tool for mastering this framework. By diligently tracking and categorizing your time investments, you gain a clear picture of where your Minutes are going and can make informed decisions to optimize your allocation. This practice not only helps you stay accountable to your goals but also provides valuable insights into your productivity patterns and areas for improvement. We'll dive deeper into the specifics of implementing a Bucket Journal in chapter 8, but for now, understand that this simple habit can revolutionize your relationship with time.

Bucket One is the "All In" bucket, where engaged Minutes offer the biggest return on your time investment. Being truly engaged and present is time well spent, even if it leads to exhaustion. The Minutes you spend fully engaged not only fulfill you in the moment but also compound in value for your future Minutes.

However, spending every Minute in Bucket One is not realistic, as it can lead to burnout. That's where Bucket Two comes in—the Limbo Bucket. Used correctly, this is where you spend Minutes reflecting on your time investment. It's a purposeful pause to take inventory and explore optimizing your time.

Bucket Three Minutes are the least valuable—the disengaged, "All Out" zone. It's tempting to wallow here, feeling worthless and hopeless. But the reality is, you will spend some Minutes here, whether you want to or not. Hitting rock bottom in Bucket Three can sometimes be the necessary catalyst to find motivation for improvement, providing the wake-up call and fuel to reengage with renewed vigor and intention.

A manager operating in Bucket Three risks derailing their entire team. When Robert replaced Dawn, many of us were headed toward Limbo, slowly slipping into disengagement. Robert tried staying All In but couldn't inspire the support to join him. Many remained lost in Limbo, gradually leaking into Bucket Three.

As a manager, achieving better time management starts with a brutally honest inventory of how you currently invest every single Minute. If you're not operating primarily in Bucket One, you can be certain your employees aren't either.

Managing a team inherently means managing their time. Your leadership either empowers your people to maximize their productivity or enables them to squander those precious Minutes. Mastering time management is one of the most critical skills you need as a leader—but first, you must master managing your own time.

Until you establish full control over your personal time investment, you'll never be equipped to effectively guide others. Once you've achieved that stability through disciplined strategies like the Bucket Journal, you can lead by example and coach your team to operate in Bucket One.

Sometimes, this harsh truth means taking the difficult path of removing those who consistently drain productivity by operating in Bucket Three. Effective time management requires making the tough choices to preserve your high performers' ability to stay fully engaged and All In. Your team's engagement, motivation, and impact ultimately flow from how you invest your own minutes as their leader. Take charge of your time, or risk watching it slip away along with your team's potential!

My experiences with Dawn and Robert were transformative, etching invaluable lessons about leadership and time management into my mind and heart. By understanding the concept of "Buckets" and consciously directing our minutes into Bucket One, we can maximize our productivity, fulfillment, and impact. As leaders, it's our responsibility to manage not only our own time but also the time of our team members. By mastering this critical skill and making tough decisions when necessary, we can create a culture of engagement and success.

Remember, every Minute matters—so make them count! Start your journey toward effective time management today by reflecting on your current habits and committing to small, consistent changes. The path to a more fulfilling, impactful life starts with a single, purposeful Minute.

CHAPTER 6

Making the Right Decisions

Clearly, Bucket One is the optimal place to invest your time. By now, you understand that—and if you're responsible for managing how other people spend their Minutes, your role is to guide them to spend their valuable time on Bucket One activities. However, notice I use the word "guide." While you can work to guide people's schedules, you can't control where people choose to invest their time.

The Importance of Decision-Making Skills

"Okay, Karen. Let's play a game of *Mommy Jeopardy*. Here is your clue: What is the one thing you want your son to know by the time he leaves for college? You have thirty seconds to provide the answer!"

I was pregnant with my first child when my dear friend Betty asked me this question. With a six-year lead time, she was happily bringing up two boys of her own. She was a successful working mom who was thrilled to share her wisdom with me. In business and at home, Betty was known for challenging the status quo with her provocative views. Even so, this question was particularly unusual, because to me the answer was a no-brainer.

"What is: I want him to know that he is loved."

"*Wrong-o*, my friend!"

Betty's booming response left me stunned, and I stared at her the way a deer stares into a pair of glaring headlights. "What do you mean?" My mind raced, unable to conjure any other valid answer.

Unfazed by the appalled look on my face, Betty said, "You want him to know how to make a great decision."

I was speechless. A great decision? Really? Are you kidding me? I opened my mouth to object. "But—"

"Hear me out, Karen. I know you won't understand this yet, but I'm giving you this view from the front lines of mother-hood. If you teach that little boy how to make a great decision, then he will know that you love him."

Betty pointed out my deeper concern before I'd had a chance to realize it myself. I had been so worried about how to make my baby feel the profound love I had for him. But if I solely focused on that feeling, I could end up smothering the little one with too much intensity. Not that I intended any harm— the love I felt for this new life was more overwhelming than anything I'd ever experienced. But maybe drowning him in that intense adoration wasn't what he needed to thrive.

And that, I realized, was the lesson Betty was trying to impart—love alone rarely equips a child with the tools for a successful, engaging adulthood. There's more to raising a well-adjusted kid than smothering them with affection. She wanted me to know that effective parenting requires a nuanced touch, careful guidance, and clear boundaries. And so it is with all effective leadership.

If I wanted to raise my son to fully engage with his life, I'd need more than acts of love. I needed to equip him with the skills to make great decisions on his own when I wasn't around to guide him. That's what real time management is about for parents and leaders alike—not just dictating how people should spend their Minutes but teaching them how to make decisions about how they spend their time.

Loving my child unconditionally would always be paramount. But ensuring he grew into someone who loved, trusted, and engaged with himself? That was the real test.

Parenting, like managing a team, isn't about rigid control. It's about providing the tools needed for people to take ownership over their personal schedules and priorities. I needed to prepare my little boy for independence, to make smart choices about how he would spend his most valuable asset.

So, what makes a great decision? Let's not overcomplicate this. A great decision is one that deposits Minutes in Bucket One.

Transitioning from Parenting to Leadership

However, it's one thing to raise a baby on the principles of time management and engagement, but it's another to bring these lessons to an adult on your team. And when you manage someone who's already well established in their ways, you'll encounter an unavoidable obstacle that can't be overlooked. It's something I call Reflective Agony.

Reflective Agony: The Nemesis to Good Decisions

Reflective Agony is a vicious cycle that can trap and paralyze you. In essence, it's the fear of altering how you spend your time because you know your habits will likely worsen before they improve. Reflective Agony happens when you stay in a boring relationship because you know that before you find a better partner, you'll spend time alone. It happens when you keep a torturous job because you would rather be disengaged than unemployed while you look for a new position. It's ignoring a new diet plan because, while you do want to lose weight, you don't want to give up ice cream or donuts.

From an outside perspective, the problem may seem obvious. If you're wasting your Minutes in Bucket Three, then a change is necessary. The sheer pain of admitting that you've been squandering your time in the wrong bucket is sometimes too daunting to handle. So, instead of experiencing the value of Minutes in Bucket One, you remain stuck in your old, unfulfilling patterns.

And the more Minutes you drop into Bucket Three, the more Reflective Agony holds you back from making a change.

When managing teams of adults, you'll often find people spiraling into the black hole of Reflective Agony. If you can't recognize the signs, you'll likely make it worse. I had to learn that the hard way.

Reflective Agony can paralyze even your most capable team members, trapping them in counterproductive habits. As a manager, you need to spot the symptoms early—the avoidance, excuses, resistance to change. Without that awareness, your efforts to course-correct could backfire, pushing them deeper into self-doubt and inaction.

Through my own stumbles, I've learned the delicate balance required when guiding those trapped in Reflective Agony. It takes empathy and resolve to help them confront their fears and break the cycle. One of my most challenging balancing acts came in the form of Allen C. Johnson.

The Story of Allen C. Johnson: A Lesson in Reflective Agony

Like me, Allen C. Johnson grew up in the '70s. However, our backgrounds could not have been further apart. Allen C.'s family lived in a New York City housing project and struggled to make ends meet. At fourteen, Allen C. joined a school release program to help pay the bills. He landed an entry-level job as a junior bank teller, and for the next twenty years, he bounced from one position in the organization to another…until he ended up on my team.

When I met Allen C., I quickly learned that the initial was an integral part of his identity. It stood for "cool"—a name he legally adopted as Allen Cool Johnson when he turned eighteen. If you wanted to grab his attention, he wouldn't turn around until he heard the "C" following his first name.

However, Allen C.'s journey at the bank was anything but cool. He suffered through two decades of misalignment, a square peg forced into a series of round holes. Despite being a diligent worker who always gave his best effort, Allen C. struggled. His lack of formal education was a constant hurdle. He wasn't cut out for his original role as a teller, so the bank shuffled him to customer service. But the fit was no better there, leading to another lateral move into loan analysis. And after floundering in that department, he was reassigned yet again to another business unit in the organization. By the time Allen C. landed on my team in the early 2000s, he had been shoehorned into nearly every division at the bank, leaving a trail of frustration in his wake.

By then, I had built a reputation as the manager who could spark engagement in any team. Those first few leadership years were electrifying—I achieved success measured not just in numbers but supercharged morale. So, when no one else could unlock Allen C.'s potential, they sent him my way.

The rest of my crew was a well-oiled machine of engaged rock stars. We obliterated projections, outshining the entire division. A finely tuned, explosive unit operating at peak performance. And then there was Allen C.—fumbling calls, bumbling accounts, and perpetually mumbling his way through meetings. He stuck out like a sore thumb amongst my all-star lineup. As a motivator of top talent, inheriting Allen C.'s long-simmering frustrations was an unprecedented challenge for me. Could I finally spark his dormant potential? Or was this hurdle too high to clear?

Allen C. was a puzzling fellow. He showed up punctually, was attentive on the surface, and always dressed in a crisp suit. But beneath that put-together exterior lurked a man crippled by two decades of unresolved Reflective Agony—and his struggle was painfully apparent. Despite his outward conscientiousness, his shoulders slumped with the weight of misalignment. His eyes were clouded by the fog of unfulfillment. For a man only in his thirties, his face carried a droop that hinted at the slow, steady downward spiral he was caught in.

The crux of Allen C.'s plight was that he was oblivious to the reality that none of his previous roles were a natural fit. He didn't know what it felt like to excel and find flow in his work. Yet he persisted, grinding away without making any real progress, unwilling or unable to break free from this cycle of Reflective Agony. He showed up and he put in the effort, but he had long ago resigned himself to a life of quiet dissatisfaction within those bank walls.

And I thought I could pull him out of it.

Oops.

After a few weeks of observing Allen C. in action, I asked him to meet me in my office. To my surprise, he showed up looking like he put real effort into his appearance that day. Instead of his standard uniform of blue jacket and black pants, Allen C. sported his favorite suit—a charcoal-gray jacket paired with tailored brown trousers. The real standout was the perfectly folded green-and-blue paisley pocket square, which brought out the flecks of color in his eyes. It was a small flourish, but it hinted at his desire to put his best foot forward. Amid the slumped shoulders and clouded gaze that had become his trademark, that jaunty pocket square was the flower in his desert, a glimmer of hope that perhaps this conversation would steer him onto a better path. I made a mental note not to judge this book too hastily.

"Allen C.," I said, "I have a new plan for you."

He drooped his head and said, "All right. You're going to send me off to a different department, aren't you."

"No, I'm not sending you anywhere else," I said. "Well, I am, but I'm not sending you out of my division. I'm sending you on a career adventure that will show you what it takes to be a great account manager."

He cocked his head, unsure of my meaning.

"Allen C., I know you want to succeed in this role," I said. "I see the effort you put into your work, but there's a disconnect—you're missing the foundational knowledge you need to support customers the way they deserve. Up until now, no one has invested in helping you develop those core skills. That's on us."

I leaned forward, maintaining eye contact. "Starting next week, I want you to attend some business classes offered through the Management Institute. We're going to expose you to knowledge, skills, and ideas that you haven't encountered yet in your career. The bank is going to support you through this—every day for the next twelve months, you'll devote at least three hours to learning something new. This is a fresh approach to 'on the job' training. The bank will cover all course fees and your regular salary while you attend classes."

A spark of encouragement flickered across his face.

I continued, "And when you've completed this program, we'll sit down and really dig into finding the right fit for your talents. This is an investment in your long-term growth and success here. You've got this, Allen C."

Allen C. beamed. "Thank you, Karen. You won't regret this."

As Allen C. walked out of my office, I felt hopeful that this could be his turning point. I knew he had some substantial gaps in his skill set, but I didn't yet recognize how wide those gaps were. Nor did I know whether this training program would actually work to bridge them, but it seemed like the right thing to do.

Up to that point, I'd operated under the assumption that Allen C. wanted this account manager role. In reality, I had no idea if he even knew what he wanted. For two decades, Allen

C. had been on autopilot, letting circumstance dictate where he ended up rather than proactively charting his own course. I didn't realize that Allen C. lacked the fundamental skills to thoughtfully choose how to spend his time. He had made one decision at fourteen out of financial necessity, and since then he'd simply stayed on that path of least resistance. He was on the Easy Road.

And with the purest of intentions, I pushed him right along.

In my eagerness to help Allen C. find fulfillment, I fell into the trap of projecting my own desires onto someone else.

Let no good deed go unpunished.

For the next year, Allen C.'s days were split between our office and the Management Institute. He diligently attended classes covering everything from formal business writing and presentation skills to competitive analysis, sales techniques, and conflict resolution—a comprehensive curriculum aimed at rounding out his professional skill set.

While he immersed himself in his courses, I strategically placed him in the business equivalent of boot camp—Allen C. was assigned a very small customer portfolio where I believed he could gain practical experience with minimal risk. This small, sectioned-off area became Allen's training grounds. I also tasked his direct manager, Darla, to keep a watchful eye on his work, just in case any issues arose.

A year into Allen C.'s intensive development program, an odd trend caught my eye in one of his top accounts. I'll refer to them as ABC Pharma. Over the previous few months, their payment volume showed a few concerning dips.

In my industry, dips like these were often an ominous sign—more often than not, they indicated a client piloting a competitor's services by redirecting a portion of their transaction flow for comparison. We'd seen this play out with other accounts in the past, and the emerging pattern with ABC Pharma set off alarm bells. Clients didn't arbitrarily test alternative providers unless they were seriously evaluating a jump to a new vendor.

I called Darla.

"I've been watching ABC Pharma for the past few months and I'm noticing some worrying trends," I said. "Since this account belongs to Allen C., I want both of you to check in with them and make sure we're meeting their needs. This will be a good learning experience for him."

A few weeks went by without any updates on the ABC Pharma situation, so I assumed my team had gotten ahead of the issue and resolved whatever caused those volume dips. That hopeful assumption was shattered when a FedEx envelope unceremoniously landed on my desk.

The letter inside was a sucker punch—ABC Pharma was terminating our services, effective immediately. According to their claims, they had tried multiple times to have a discussion with us about their pricing and servicing concerns. Despite their outreach efforts, no one followed up to address their needs. They felt they had no choice but to sever ties and take their business elsewhere.

I stared at that letter, a pit forming in my stomach and steam building in my ears. Not only had we potentially lost a major client account, but it had happened right under Allen C.'s watch during a critical phase of his professional development. All the training, all the investment in expanding his skills…and we still dropped the ball in a spectacular way.

What a wake-up call. For all his progress, Allen C. had still failed to develop the intuitive client management and communication skills required to tend to his accounts. Worse, the lapse exposed an accountability gap—had Darla also dropped the ball in overseeing his work?

I snatched up my phone and punched in Darla's number.

"I'm holding a termination letter from ABC Pharma. I asked you to work with Allen C. to investigate those volume dips. Help me understand this!" I fumed.

"I'm not sure what happened," she said, "Allen C. swore he handled it…"

My breath caught, and I could feel my face turning red with fury.

"What do you mean, he handled it? Did you go with him to visit the customer or not?"

"Well, no," she said. "I had a conflict, and Allen C. was confident he could take care of it. I know how hard he's been working on those classes and I thought—"

"Get him on the phone, please," I said through gritted teeth.

A few clicks later, Allen C. joined the call.

"Hello?" he said.

"Allen, I'm sitting here staring at a termination letter for the ABC Pharma account. They're leaving."

"Oh," Allen C. said, "I know."

"You know?"

"Yes, ma'am," he said. "They actually called me a few weeks ago and told me."

I rubbed my forehead. "So this news is not a surprise to you?"

"No, it's not," he said. "I knew they were leaving."

I took a deep breath, trying to keep my composure. "Allen C., why didn't you tell anyone? Why didn't you let me or Darla know that we were at risk of losing this account?"

There was a long pause on the other end of the line. "I don't know," he finally said. "I guess I just didn't want to bother you with it. I thought I could handle it on my own."

The Consequences of Reflective Agony

And there it was—the crux of Allen C.'s struggle, laid bare. Even after a year of intensive training and support, he still lacked the confidence and initiative to proactively address client concerns. He was so paralyzed by the fear of failure, so trapped in the cycle of Reflective Agony, that he couldn't bring himself to ask for help when he needed it most.

It was a painful realization, but one I couldn't ignore. Despite my best efforts, Allen C. wasn't thriving in this role. The training program, while well intentioned, hadn't been enough to bridge the fundamental gaps in his skill set and mindset. He was still stuck on the Easy Road, letting circumstances dictate his outcomes rather than taking ownership of his decisions and actions.

I knew then that it was time for a difficult conversation. Prolonging this mismatch would only lead to more frustration and disappointment for everyone involved. Allen C. needed a fresh start, a chance to find his true calling outside the confines of the bank.

Three days later, I visited ABC Pharma to apologize for our poor performance and receive their highly critical feedback. Once the meeting was over, I walked back to our corporate headquarters and accomplished the task that no one at the bank had the courage to do for twenty years: I fired Allen C. Johnson.

While walking him to the elevators, his box of belongings in my hands, I tried to explain my decision to him.

"You'll be fine, Allen C.," I said. "You're a hard worker. This just isn't the place for you. I know you'll land on your feet someday soon. Who knows, maybe one day you'll even thank me for this."

"I doubt it," he mumbled. "This is the end for me, Karen. This is all I've ever known."

He took his box from me, stepped into the elevator, and tried to keep a brave face while the elevator doors closed.

Breaking Free from the Easy Road

Three years went by without a word from Allen C. Johnson. Then, one bright Chicago morning, I was on a conference call when my secretary barged in, urgently mouthing that someone needed to speak with me. Fearing a crisis with my family, I excused myself and grabbed the phone, trepidation building. The voice on the other end was the last I expected.

"Karen? It's Allen C…Allen C. Johnson."

"Hi, Allen C.," I said hesitantly.

I didn't know what to expect from his call. I thought maybe he called to tell me he was still miserable and jobless, or worse, to ask for his job back. I half expected him to tell me he'd sabotaged my house. Instead, he asked me a question.

"Do you remember what you told me three years ago when you fired me?"

I settled into my chair, intrigued and admittedly apprehensive about where this conversation was headed.

I thought for a moment. "That one day you'd thank me?"

"You are exactly right, and that day is today, Karen. Thank you. You know, I was really torn up after you let me go. I spent a month feeling sorry for myself. But then I thought, *Well,*

maybe she's right. Maybe there is something better out there for me.
So I applied for a sales job at Veri-Mobile, and they hired me to
sell cellular phone plans to big companies like the ones at the
bank. And Karen, I have to say, it's just perfect! All that training
and schooling I did at the bank came together here. I'm the top
salesman at the company. They've even asked me to lead my
own team. I'm headed to the Bahamas next month for Presi-
dent's Club since I smashed all my quotas. When I was working
for the bank, I didn't know that a job like this existed. And if
you hadn't fired me, I never would. I finally found my place."

I was stunned. I tried to think of something smart to say,
but eventually, I simply said my first thought out loud: "God
bless you, Allen C. I'm so happy for you."

"Me too, Karen. Thank you again."

Allen C.'s story is a powerful reminder of the dangers of
Reflective Agony and the Easy Road. When we let fear and
inertia dictate our choices, we rob ourselves of the opportunity
to find true fulfillment and engagement in our work and lives.
It takes courage and self-awareness to break free from those
patterns, but the rewards are immeasurable.

Applying the Lessons to Your Own Life and Leadership

As leaders, it's our responsibility to help our team members
navigate these challenges. We must be attuned to the signs of
Reflective Agony and the Easy Road and be willing to have the
tough conversations when necessary. It's not about rigid control
or dictating how people spend their time but rather about providing the tools and guidance they need to make great decisions
for themselves.

Here are a few key takeaways to consider:

1. Regularly assess whether you and your team members are investing time in Bucket One activities. If not, dig deeper to understand the root causes and take action to realign priorities.
2. Be vigilant for signs of Reflective Agony, such as avoidance, excuses, or resistance to change. When spotted, approach the issue with empathy and resolve, helping team members confront their fears and break the cycle.
3. Recognize when you or a team member is on the Easy Road, letting circumstances dictate outcomes rather than proactively making decisions. Encourage a shift toward intentional, purposeful action.
4. When a fundamental mismatch exists between an individual and their role, have the courage to make a clean break. Prolonging misalignment benefits no one in the long run.
5. Model the behavior you wish to see in your team. Demonstrate a commitment to investing in Bucket One activities, making tough decisions when necessary, and continuously learning and growing.

The path to fulfillment and engagement is rarely a straight line. It's a journey filled with twists, turns, and the occasional detour. But by equipping ourselves and our teams with the tools to make great decisions, we can navigate those challenges with confidence and purpose.

Remember, a single purposeful Minute invested in the right activities can change the trajectory of a life. As leaders, it's our privilege and responsibility to help others find and embrace those Minutes, one decision at a time.

CHAPTER 7

Overcoming Obstacles to Change

Acknowledging the need for change doesn't guarantee execution. It's one step to recognize that your Minutes are not all going into Bucket One. It's another step entirely to make a change. When the time comes to make a substantial shift—whether it's leaving a company, relocating to a new neighborhood, or ending a relationship—several insidious factors can thwart your ability to follow through.

To illustrate this point, let's take a closer look at the story of my good friend, John P. John P. is one of the most remarkable people I've had the privilege of knowing. He played an integral role in the creation of the Three Bucket Philosophy. But, as you might suspect, it wasn't always that way.

When I first met John, I was in the midst of a transition to a new bank. John's genuine enthusiasm for his work and his encyclopedic knowledge of the organization immediately caught my eye. The Three Bucket Philosophy was a foreign concept to him at the time, but his principles aligned with its goals. He already spent most of his Minutes on Bucket One pursuits.

As the US Eastern Region sales manager, John was a force of nature. He was in the trenches with his people, maintaining a steady presence during joint customer calls. When it came to winning new business, he was a brilliant strategist. And through his team's darkest times he was an unwavering pillar of support, whether it was the loss of a family member or a difficult medical diagnosis. John was more than just a manager; he was his team's guardian angel.

John's dedication to his work and his team was unparalleled. When other groups needed help, John was the first to raise his hand. He dove in to train new staff and introduce cutting-edge product solutions, and he threw the most epic after-hours get-togethers. But his passion for helping others didn't stop there. John poured his heart and soul into educating disadvantaged teens and young adults, arming them with the life skills they needed to succeed.

When I met John, he was a shining example of a life well lived. He married his college sweetheart, and together they built a family with two adorable girls. He gave freely, without expecting anything in return, and the universe rewarded him in spades—not just with financial abundance, but with the priceless gifts of peace, love, and happiness. To be in John's presence was to be enveloped in a magnetic field of positive energy, and everyone who crossed his path couldn't help but be inspired by his unwavering spirit.

However, despite John's seemingly perfect life, a storm was brewing on the horizon. Though John was content with the status quo, the bank's leadership had a different vision. My primary role was to help the bank navigate its transformation journey, and I wasn't alone in this effort. Several new faces joined the ranks a few months after my arrival, including a fresh leader for John's department. She was a holdover manager, assigned only to help John's department navigate the new changes streaming down from the C-suite.

John's new manager brought with her a whirlwind of change—new objectives, alternative ways of thinking, and unconventional approaches to raising productivity quotas. Whether the change was good or bad is debatable, but the implementation was chaos. Floor-to-ceiling renovations swept through the office, project timelines were fast-tracked, and opposing viewpoints were snuffed out. The workplace was effectively turned on its head.

In an instant, most of John's coworkers were running for the hills, resignation letters in hand, and his comfortable world was upended.

The impact on John was devastating. A profound sense of loss weighed over him. The world he once knew, the one where he thrived and made a profound impact, disappeared. He was lost in a new and unfamiliar environment.

As he sat at his desk, the one he occupied for fifteen years, he looked around an office he hardly recognized. Dark boxes on the walls marked where his motivational posters used to hang. Empty desks and chairs cluttered the open floor—remains of those who'd fled from this new manager's rule. Flickering fluorescent lights made the place seem haunted. The role that had once felt like a dream come true now resembled a stark, gray nightmare.

Faced with this harsh reality, John could no longer ignore the truth. He was disengaged. He was burnt out. The time he spent at work had lost its meaning, and the realization hit him like a punch in the gut. He was suffering, and the remnants of his team were suffering. If he didn't act soon, they'd all lose themselves.

There were no easy options, but John knew he couldn't stay put. He refused to be trapped in this gray purgatory, watching his Minutes waste away. He had to find a way forward, not just for himself, but for the sake of his team, and for the impact he wanted to make in the world. The time had come to embrace the unknown.

But what next?

John took a leap of faith. He made a decision he believed would be the key to reengaging with his purpose. It was a courageous move, a step toward change, but tragically, his choice only plunged him deeper into endless cycles of frustration and despair.

He decided to double down.

John thought he could bring his team around. He believed he could bend reality to his will and that he could force everyone's engagement and satisfaction back to its former glory. This was John's fatal flaw.

As the months passed under the new manager's harsh rule, John struggled to maintain his composure. His patience, empathy, and compassion waned. He started ending team meetings with the hollow mantra, "I know this is tough, but we don't have a choice here." He sent out teamwide emails in all caps, demanding results he could send upstream. He no longer asked for his team's cooperation—he barked orders, dismissed problems, and ignored complaints.

Just a few more months of this, John told himself, *and someone new will come along. Everything will eventually go back to normal. I can do this. We can do this. We can't quit.*

But despite John's best efforts, the situation only worsened. Desperation wrapped itself around John and his team. Goals were met, but with considerable struggle. John thought he was reengaging, but in reality he was only disengaging further. His passion and enthusiasm eroded from the relentless pressure bearing down from above him, and he became a mere shadow of the man he once was. John, a once vibrant and engaged employee, slogged through his days without any sense of purpose or fulfillment.

I can't fault John for fighting. No one can. But if I could go back in time and tell him one thing during this struggle, I would have said, "John, you're a ferocious warrior, but you're fighting for the wrong cause. You're clinging to a world that no longer exists. Knock it off!"

Unfortunately, time machines have yet to be invented.

John's story is not unique. He was just like many mid-career employees, carrying the weight of a mortgage, monthly bills, and the ever-increasing burden of his kids' school tuition. The thought of losing his steady paycheck was more terrifying than the living nightmare he was stuck in. So, he stayed at work, pushing himself to the point of exhaustion.

John's breaking point came when he least expected it: at three o'clock in the morning, in Las Vegas, when he happened to look in the mirror.

John was no stranger to Las Vegas, having attended the annual industry trade show in Sin City many times before. Normally he looked forward to the opportunity to network with colleagues and meet with high-value clients. But this year, as he prepared for the trip, his usual excitement was conspicuously absent.

On the morning of his departure, John received an email. It contained the results of his recent performance review. The word "INCONSISTENT" glared at him, a far cry from the

"STRONG PERFORMER" rating he'd regularly earned over his fifteen-year career.

And INCONSISTENT meant two things: one, your annual bonus was gone. And two…you're now at the top of the list for the next round of corporate layoffs.

Have a great time in Vegas, John! Keep up the terrible work!

John was devastated. As he boarded a crowded plane, he wedged himself into his middle seat and cradled his head in his hands for the entire flight. By the time he landed, he had two massive sties, one on each eye.

The night before the conference, John's eyes were in such excruciating pain that sleep eluded him. Desperate for guidance, he reached for his phone and dialed his wife's number, relying more on muscle memory than sight to punch in the digits. As the phone rang, John felt a sense of despair wash over him.

"I look like Rocky Racoon, Jax! My eyes are on fire. I'm supposed to meet clients tomorrow, but I can't see anything. What am I going to do?"

"The internet says to put a warm compress on it. I'm sorry, honey."

John flailed around for a washcloth and ran it under the hotel bathroom sink. He pressed it to his eyes when the water ran warm.

"Any better?" asked Jax.

John pressed on the cloth, waiting for some sense of relief. It only took a few moments for him to realize the severity of his situation.

"How did it get this bad?" he said.

"This site says it's an infection," Jax replied.

But John wasn't talking about his eyes. He was referring to the sight staring back at him in the mirror, the man squinting through two swollen, stinging eyes. Despite his lack of vision, John's situation had never been more clear: it was time to make a change.

For the past year, John had refused to acknowledge the toll his job took on his mental and physical well-being. He pushed through the stress, the anxiety, and the growing sense of dissatisfaction, convincing himself that he could handle it, that things would get better. But now, as he stared straight at the results of his effort, he could no longer ignore the effects of his struggle.

In that moment of painful clarity, John knew he had reached a turning point. He had lost his way, veering off the path of fulfillment and purpose that had once guided his career. The realization was a painful one, but it was also a moment of clarity, a wake-up call that he was long overdue.

As he stood in the harsh light of the hotel bathroom, John knew that he had a choice to make. He could continue down the path he was on, ignoring the warning signs and pushing through the pain, or he could take a hard look at his life and make a change.

The realization was hard to acknowledge. But sometimes, it takes hitting rock bottom to finally break free from what holds us back. So, with a heavy heart and a newfound sense of determination, John resolved to take the first step on that journey: he left Las Vegas to look for a new opportunity.

John's experience is a powerful reminder that countless people have faced similar "How did it get this bad?" moments. However, the answers are often painfully clear. The Easy Road has plenty of warning signs, but the detour to the Hard Road is scary. After all, it's much easier to "grind it out" in a current job, relationship, or neighborhood than to face unemployment, singleness, or a physical move.

The more time people spend hesitating to make a change, the more precious Minutes they squander. Those who choose the path of least resistance, coasting down the Easy Road, inevitably find themselves back on the Hard Road, bogged down by the consequences of their inaction. They may find themselves terminated for subpar performance, struggling in their marriage under the weight of neglect, or abandoned by friends who can no longer tolerate their incessant work-related rants. They find themselves pouring Minutes into Bucket Three, and that is a miserable place for Minutes to be.

The longer people remain in Bucket Three, the more their negativity and dissatisfaction seep into every aspect of their lives, poisoning their relationships and eroding their sense of self-worth. It's a vicious cycle, one that can be tough to break free from without conscious effort and a willingness to confront difficult truths.

But the alternative—watching helplessly as one's time plinks away into Minutes Hell—is far worse. It's a slow death, a gradual erosion of the soul that leaves people hollow and unfulfilled, wondering where their passion and purpose have gone.

The key to saving yourself from such a fate is to recognize the signs early. Listen to that nagging voice in the back of your mind that whispers, *This isn't right. This isn't where I'm meant to be.* It takes courage to heed that call, to step off the Easy Road and onto the path of change. But every Minute spent in Bucket Three is a Minute wasted, a lost opportunity to live with meaning and fulfillment.

Change is hard. Quitting is hard. Standing up for yourself and your Minutes is hard.

Deciding to alter the way you spend your Minutes is the first step toward becoming a Three Bucket Leader, but the decision alone is insufficient. Once you begin the work of transforming your time-spending habits, you may experience some initial improvements, but you will likely encounter obstacles to long-term change.

To be a Three Bucket Leader, you must recognize the barriers to change and develop strategies to overcome them. Through my experience, I have identified three primary obstacles: rose-colored glasses, delusional procrastination, and tunnel vision. Each of these impediments, if left unchecked, can prevent you or your employees from making the necessary changes, even when the need for change is clear.

Rose-colored glasses refers to the tendency to view past experiences and current situations through an overly optimistic lens, minimizing the negative aspects and exaggerating the positive. This distorted perspective can lead individuals to cling to outdated habits and resist change, convincing themselves the status quo is better than it actually is.

Delusional procrastination is the habit of continually putting off necessary changes, convincing yourself that the "right time" to take action is always just around the corner. This mindset can lead to a perpetual state of inaction, where individuals remain stuck in unproductive patterns of behavior, always waiting for the perfect moment to make a change that never arrives.

Finally, **tunnel vision** describes the narrow focus that develops when people become so consumed by their daily tasks and responsibilities, they lose sight of the bigger picture. This limited perspective can make it difficult to recognize the need for change, as well as the potential benefits that come from altering negative time-spending habits.

To be an effective Three Bucket Leader, you must be aware of these obstacles and actively work to overcome them. By developing strategies to combat rose-colored glasses, delusional procrastination, and tunnel vision, you can create an environment that fosters positive, lasting change, both for yourself and for those you lead.

Rose-Colored Glasses

One of the most significant factors holding people back from change is their own nostalgia. It's the same feeling that gripped John when he resisted leaving his post, even though the job he once loved had become a nightmare. His dream job disappeared in his rearview mirror, yet he held on, unwilling to let go of the memory. The nostalgia for his former position had a powerful hold on him.

When most people start a new job, they're excited. A new job feels like a whole new world, brimming with opportunities to learn, grow, and succeed. New employees are eager to tackle new challenges, share innovative ideas, and forge meaningful relationships with their colleagues. It's as if they're viewing their new workplace through a pair of rose-colored glasses, seeing their new adventure tinted pink with promise.

While the job might feel engaging at first, jobs change over time. New managers appear. New team dynamics form. New initiatives slowly change the shape of a position. Plus, the flaws and challenges that were always present but initially overlooked become harder to ignore. The perfect candidate for a role may not fit it as well as it grows to include new processes, technology, and responsibilities. Sometimes people grow out of jobs...and sometimes jobs outgrow people.

When you start a new job, your excitement and optimism can act like a pair of rose-colored glasses, making even a less than ideal situation (Bucket Three) appear as though it's your dream job (Bucket One). However, just like wearing colored glasses, the initial euphoria eventually fades as your brain adapts to the new reality. Over time, your mind becomes accustomed to the "filtered" view of your job, and you begin to perceive the rosy, romantic view as "normal." You might not even realize you're still looking at your work through the lens of your initial expectations and enthusiasm. The metaphorical glasses remain in place, continuing to influence your perception, even if you're no longer consciously aware of their presence.

It's only when you take a step back and remove these rose-colored glasses that you can appreciate how much your outlook was altered. Suddenly, you can see your job for what it really is. This revelation can be eye-opening as you come to terms with the romanticization of your reality.

Recognizing the power of these rose-colored glasses is essential for making informed decisions about your career. By acknowledging that your perception can be influenced by your initial expectations and emotions, you can strive to assess your work more objectively. This awareness allows you to separate the reality of your job from the idealized version you may have initially embraced, enabling you to make choices that align with your true goals and values.

Choosing to leave a job means choosing to leave the glasses behind. It means recognizing you're not giving your brain a full spectrum of information and accepting that you chose to keep your perception behind a filter. Taking off the glasses requires humility, forgiveness, and vulnerability. For most, this is an emotionally painful experience.

To avoid this trap, it's crucial to regularly take a step back and objectively assess your situation. By doing so, you can identify any mismatches between your expectations and reality, giving you the power to make informed decisions that align with your goals and values. Recognizing when it's time to change course is key.

While it may be comforting to maintain a positive outlook on our job, it's essential to acknowledge when it's necessary to move in a new direction. By doing this, you ensure that your career choices are based on a realistic understanding of your circumstances. Adopting this approach allows you to navigate your professional journey with greater clarity and purpose, ultimately leading to a more fulfilling and successful career.

Delusional Procrastination

"After this deadline, everything will snap back to normal."

"I really need to find a new job. But then I remember the mortgage, the bills, and the uncertainty of the job market. So, I swallow my pride, paste on a fake smile, and continue this charade, hoping that one day I'll find the courage to break free."

"We just have to make it over this one last hurdle."

"As much as I despise it, leaving now would mean starting from scratch, and I'm not sure I have the energy for that anymore."

"If we can just finish this last push, things will look much better for us."

You've likely heard these things before. Perhaps you've even said them yourself. These phrases are born of an ever-extending ladder, when each success at work is met with a new, more challenging task. All the stress, pain, and unrealistic expectations you've endured becomes the new normal. After all, if you've done it once, you're expected to do it again and again, without relief. This relentless climb leaves you drained, both physically and emotionally, as you struggle to meet growing demands. You want to say, "Enough!" but you somehow believe you're right near the end...so, you hold out.

Delusional procrastination doesn't prevent you from reaching the finish line. Instead, it stops you from crossing the "I'm finished" line—the point at which you finally decide to call it quits. No matter how quickly you approach this line, you'll never reach it as long as you're under the illusion that your disengagement is temporary.

This is the second most common obstacle people face when trying to improve their engagement: the misguided belief that if they simply hold on until a particular task or project is complete, their job will snap back into place like a rubber band, and they'll feel engaged once more. However, this is rarely the case. In truth, they're only delaying the inevitable and wasting precious time in the process.

In a way, this obstacle resembles the rose-colored glasses analogy. In both situations, you instinctively know something is amiss. However, when wearing rose-colored glasses, you remain in your job due to a sense of attachment. This is where delusional procrastination differs.

With delusional procrastination, you're not attached to the job. In fact, you want it to end. Nevertheless, your fear of change outweighs your fear of staying the same, so you choose the path of least resistance.

John's manager completely drained his engagement levels, and yet he didn't leave. He clung to the belief that with the right approach, the right numbers, and the right plan, he could win her over. More importantly, he feared that leaving would only exacerbate his other problems. With a family to support and a mortgage to pay, he chose what he believed to be the lesser of two evils. His delusion morphed into literal momentary blindness as he resisted the inevitable, refusing to acknowledge the reality of his situation.

When your Minutes are consistently landing in Bucket Three, it's impossible to shift them back into Bucket One without making a significant change. They don't end up in Bucket Three by chance. There are underlying reasons for their placement. Regardless of how desperately you want your Minutes to return to Bucket One, if you resist change, you're engaging in delusional procrastination.

Delusional procrastinators have a problematic tendency to confuse disengagement with busyness. There's nothing inherently wrong with being busy at work—in fact, for those spending Minutes in Bucket One, being busy often means maximizing their time—but for disengaged individuals, being busy translates to constantly pushing their own healthy boundaries. Rather than maximize their time, they maximize their misery, trudging through daily tasks without a sense of purpose. Engaged busy Minutes are valuable, but Minutes spent postponing the inevitable are not.

It's essential to recognize you can't delude yourself into believing your job will improve without any meaningful effort on your part. In some cases, even significant efforts—such as setting new workplace boundaries, adjusting tasks, or having open conversations with leadership—may not be sufficient to bring about change. By all means, do your best to turn your job around, but if you don't see the desired results, you can't continue to procrastinate making a change.

Tunnel Vision

While the two previously mentioned obstacles are obvious problems, this final obstacle is a problem masquerading as a solution. This is because tunnel vision takes the form of something most people would consider to be a positive thing: a clearly defined goal. The issue with tunnel vision is that the clearly defined goal is, in fact, Bucket Three.

It may appear illogical for someone to consciously set Bucket Three as their goal, but it occurs more frequently than you might expect, and under fairly common circumstances. Consider a scenario where your dream job starts to devour all your available time. In addition to the standard eight hours, you find yourself working evenings, weekends, and holidays. Initially, this doesn't feel like an issue because the work is novel and exciting, and offers a chance to acquire new skills and knowledge. However, as the learning opportunities diminish, you become drained by the repetitive and monotonous nature of the job.

As the work becomes routine and mechanical, the value of your time diminishes. When this happens, your Bucket One Minutes are diverted into Buckets Two and Three. What began as an opportunity to go above and beyond—because you wanted to do this—gradually becomes a new expectation, which then becomes the new norm. One weekend shift to make a deadline push turns into Saturdays at the office. Paperwork you filled out to help an overloaded colleague suddenly becomes part of your daily tasks.

There's a difference between putting in extra effort because you want to and pushing yourself to the limit because you have to. The former is driven by passion and personal growth, while the latter is fueled by obligation and external pressure. There's no quicker way to burn out than to repeatedly stretch beyond your capacity.

The more unstimulating you find your work, the worse you'll feel about your days. It feels like every day starts and ends the same way, and the clock is not your friend. You arrive at work at 8:00 a.m. and spend the majority of the morning and afternoon watching the slow progression of your desk clock, counting down the minutes until you can leave. You crave a new, novel kind of work, something exciting and more closely aligned with your personal interests.

Your solution is to find a new job, but you must be cautious. Before making a change, it's essential to think critically about what is making you feel disengaged. Is it the job itself, your manager, your workplace, or a loss of faith in your company? You must identify where the disconnect lies before you make a move, or you risk running into the same problems in a new environment. Same room, different furniture. Same song, different band.

When you decide to change, your next move must be aligned with what you want, not what you think you should want. Unfortunately, very few people can pinpoint the root cause of their dissatisfaction until someone else bluntly tells them to think about what they really want.

Tunnel vision may lead you to believe you need the exact same position at a new company. A new company may boast a better workplace culture, provide a more competitive salary, and offer a more comprehensive benefits package, but will the new position reignite your passion for your work? Once you adapt to the change in pay and the initial excitement of the new environment fades, will you genuinely enjoy what you're doing?

This is the tunnel vision problem: once you decide to change companies without engaging in some introspection about why you're making the change, you charge down a new wrong path. You still feel a sense of hope, and you still believe you're taking back control of your life, but in reality, you're just exchanging one set of problems for another. You're not addressing the underlying issues that led to your dissatisfaction in the first place.

To avoid falling into the tunnel vision trap, it's crucial to take a step back and assess your situation objectively. Ask yourself tough questions about what you truly want from your career. What aspects of your current job do you enjoy, and which ones drain your energy? What kind of work environment allows you to thrive? What values and goals are most important to you?

By engaging in this self-reflection, you can gain a clearer understanding of what you need to feel fulfilled in your work. Armed with this knowledge, you can make more informed decisions about your career path, ensuring that your next move aligns with your true desires and aspirations.

Applying the Lessons to Your Own Life and Leadership

As a leader, it's essential to recognize these obstacles not only in your own life but also in the lives of those you lead. By understanding the challenges that can hinder positive change, you can better support your team members as they navigate their own professional journeys.

Here are five key takeaways for applying these lessons to your life and leadership:

1. Regularly assess your situation objectively. Take off the rose-colored glasses and evaluate your job, relationships, and overall life satisfaction with a critical eye. Encourage your team members to do the same, creating a culture of self-awareness and growth.

2. Recognize the difference between being busy and being engaged. Don't fall into the trap of delusional procrastination, convincing yourself that things will improve on their own. If you or your team members are consistently spending Minutes in Bucket Three, take action to address the underlying issues.

3. Identify the root causes of dissatisfaction. When considering a change, dig deep to understand what's truly driving your discontent. Help your team members do the same, encouraging them to reflect on their values, goals, and aspirations.

4. Align your decisions with your true desires. Don't let tunnel vision lead you down the wrong path. Make career choices that genuinely align with what you want, not what you think you should want. Support your team members in doing the same, fostering a culture of authenticity and purpose.

5. Seek help when needed. Overcoming these obstacles can be challenging, and it's okay to ask for support. Whether it's seeking guidance from a mentor, working with a coach, or simply having open conversations with trusted colleagues, don't hesitate to reach out for help when you need it. As a leader, model this

behavior and create a safe space for your team members to do the same.

By incorporating these lessons into your own life and leadership, you can break free from the obstacles that prevent positive change and create a more fulfilling, purposeful existence for yourself and those you lead. Remember, change is rarely easy, but it's always worth it when it means aligning your Minutes with your true values and aspirations.

As you continue on your journey as a Three Bucket Leader, keep these lessons in mind. Recognize the power of rose-colored glasses, the dangers of delusional procrastination, and the pitfalls of tunnel vision. By staying vigilant and proactive, you can overcome these obstacles and create a life and career that truly reflects your authentic self.

In the next chapter, we'll explore the importance of setting boundaries and saying no to protect your Minutes and ensure they're spent in a way that aligns with your goals and values. As a leader, this skill is essential not only for your own well-being but also for the success and engagement of your team. By learning to set clear boundaries and communicate them effectively, you can create a more positive, productive, and fulfilling work environment for everyone involved.

CHAPTER 8

Balancing Your Buckets

Imagine sitting down to review your finances and realizing someone has been stealing from you. Every day, someone you trusted to manage your money has stolen fifty dollars a day for *years*, right under your nose. You'd be furious! I know I would be. That money adds up. If I learned that was happening to me, I'd fight tooth and nail to get my money back. And I certainly would never trust that thieving miscreant within a mile of my finances ever again.

Now instead of someone stealing money from you, imagine they're stealing your time. As you reflect on the past few years, you come to a startling realization: countless Minutes, perhaps even thousands, have vanished from your allotted twenty-four hours a day. These precious moments have slipped through your fingers, never to be reclaimed. The harsh truth is that time, once lost, can never be recovered. There's no insurance policy that can compensate for the Minutes taken from you, no way to turn back the clock and regain what has been lost.

To make matters worse, you know there's only one person who could possibly have stolen that time...and it's you.

When you find out you've been losing time in Bucket Three, brace yourself for an emotional roller coaster. Self-loathing, shame, sadness, regret, and fear—they'll all come crashing over you. You might even start doubting yourself. Don't hide from these feelings—they're real and they're valid. But here's the thing: don't let them freeze you in your tracks, either. Feel them, acknowledge them, and then prepare yourself to keep moving forward.

After my husband showed me the video of my dark, harrowing performance that night at the restaurant, I was furious. Not at him, but at myself. I didn't recognize that woman on the iPad. She was a stranger to me, and I despised her. She wasn't the person I wanted to be. She didn't live the values I held so dear. She was a thief, and she was stealing my precious Minutes.

Accepting the person I had become was hard to digest. However, regaining control of my time meant reconciling my past and present selves. I had to admit to my detour away from Bucket One, squandering my Minutes in the very bucket I warned my team, family, and friends against—the bucket of wasted time. The responsibility was mine, and mine alone.

Hypocrisy stared me in the face—I was living the very lifestyle I cautioned against. What a tragic disappointment. Fortunately, I knew the cure: a dose of my own medicine. It was time to stand up for my Minutes and make the necessary change.

So, I left the job I loved.

Leaving my role was a deliberate decision, one that was made swiftly but not without serious thought. To be a genuine Three Bucket Leader, I needed to focus my energy on what mattered most to me. This required a fresh perspective to reignite my own engagement. Parting ways with my company was challenging, but it was the best decision I could have made.

I often find myself reminiscing about the dynamic energy of the banking world—the fast pace, the pressure, the rewarding challenge of delivering exceptional results to clients, and the joy I felt from empowering my team. I knew I needed a change of scenery to rediscover myself, but I didn't want to lose the elements of my work I loved.

Stepping away from the job gave me the space I needed to reassess how to invest my time and energy. This reflection ultimately led me to the consulting world, where I gained greater autonomy to choose how I allocate my time. This newfound freedom allowed me to reconnect with my passions and pursue a more fulfilling professional life.

Rediscovering my purpose as a workplace engagement consultant has been a transformative experience. Each new client brings a unique set of challenges, and I feel an overwhelming sense of fulfillment in every new case. Helping leaders, employees, and individuals from all walks of life discover their own sense of purpose is incredibly rewarding, and it fuels my dedication to this work.

Initially, this rediscovery was invigorating, like a blazing bonfire engulfing every inch of kindling with bright, fierce flames. However, as that fire settled into a steady, consistent burn, I recognized the possibility of losing sight of my goals and flickering out once more if I was not attentive.

While I advise plenty of clients on their workplace engagement, I also recognize that I need my own strategy to keep my Minutes in Bucket One. I can't always depend on external factors, like my husband capturing my restaurant rants, to hold me accountable. Instead, I require a more sustainable method to maintain my commitment to my purpose, one that helps me ensure this next chapter of my life is the best one yet.

That's why I started the Bucket Journal.

Formulating the Bucket Journal

Before the Bucket Journal, I struggled to prioritize journaling in my life. I know how beneficial journaling is, but I always felt like I was too busy to sit down and record my own thoughts. Even though I wanted to make journaling a habit, it always seemed to fall to the bottom of my ever-growing to-do list.

When I changed careers, I gained back some time I used to reevaluate my priorities. I realized that self-reflection was the only way I could remain true to myself. Slowly but surely, I incorporated journaling into my daily routine. Now, writing my thoughts down on paper is an essential part of my daily routine. It calms my mind and helps me process my experiences. It's a practice that works well for me, and I believe everyone can benefit from some form of self-reflection and journaling. The key is to find a method that resonates with you, whether it's traditional pen and paper, digital notes, voice recordings, or some other format that allows you to express your thoughts and feelings.

Journaling is a great way to rebuild trust. If you know you've been throwing away a significant portion of your Minutes into Bucket Three, it can be challenging to trust your own decision-making skills. You might find yourself wondering how to ensure that you're being responsible with your Minutes and not inadvertently putting them into Bucket Three. This is where journaling can be incredibly helpful.

When I first started journaling, my approach was simple and straightforward. I would:

1. Open my Bible to a random page and read.
2. Pray.
3. Write down my reflections in my journal.

At first, this basic method served me well. However, I soon discovered that while the practice was helpful for centering myself, it wasn't helping me keep track of how I spent my time, and my Minutes seemed to slip away unnoticed. To tackle this issue, I decided to incorporate an extra step into my journaling routine, which eventually led to the creation of the Bucket Journal.

The new fourth step in my journaling routine was to conclude each day by rating its events on a scale of 1 to 3, with 1 being the best and 3 being the worst. Interestingly, I have never actually given myself a perfect score of 1 because, in my mind, that represents an absolutely flawless day. To maintain my own sense of integrity, the highest score I allow myself is 1.1. This isn't a strict rule but rather a personal choice I make. After all, there's always room for improvement, right?

This additional step helped me understand where I spent my Minutes on a daily basis. I could see how small, seemingly innocent Bucket Two and Three tasks added up to create middling days. I could also see how days that felt lackluster were actually packed with Bucket One moments. The more I kept track of my time, the better I could plan for how to spend the next day. I became more conscious of my personal growth journey through little moments of self-reflection.

By assigning a numerical value to my Minutes during my evening journaling sessions, I slowly regained confidence in my decision-making process. The scores served as a tangible reflection of my state of mind and provided a consistent measure for my Minutes. The lower the number, the more satisfied I felt with the choices I made throughout the day.

For a long time, this approach worked well. Scores of 1.2, 1.35, 1.15, 1.5, 1.22, etc., filled my journal. Each day ended with a sense of accomplishment. This feeling gave me the freedom to wake up the next day, fired up for life, knowing that I was still spending my Minutes in Bucket One!

I was All In! I was living my purpose! I was happy!

Then one day I scored a 2.4.

Aww, darn it!

I woke up the next day feeling sad and doubtful, as if I had lost valuable momentum. Even worse, I lost confidence in myself. I began to question whether I was veering off course once again. Did I need to pivot away from consulting? If I felt like my Minutes were being divided between Bucket Two and Bucket Three, surely that meant I needed to make a change, didn't it?

The next afternoon, I had a video call with one of my peers. We'll call him Ray.

"What's going on, Karen? How are you?"

"Well, Ray, I'm in a bad place. I'm in a really bad frame of mind."

"Oh no! That's not like you! What's wrong?"

I thought about the question objectively for a moment. Was it the bad Bucket Journal getting me down? Or something else?

"I'll tell you what's wrong, Ray. Yesterday I scored a 2.4."

Ray nodded. He knew I was referring to my Bucket Journal. *"What do you think gave you that score?"* he asked.

"Two things," I said. "First, I had an absolutely terrible meeting with a client. You know me, Ray, I love my clients. But this guy…I just knew he was going to take advantage of my time. And after waiting in his office for thirty minutes he finally came out and said, 'Sorry, I forgot. Can we reschedule?' It made me furious! We rescheduled, but I don't think I want to keep this person as a client.

"The second was a call with my son. He wants me to support a decision he's making, but I don't agree with his thinking. I feel he's headed in the wrong direction, so I told him that. Well, he didn't take it well. We hung up and didn't talk for several hours. When we spoke again we were able to clear the air, but still, I felt *bad*. I felt like I was forcing my opinion instead of offering my perspective."

"How much time did the meeting with that client and the call with your son take?" Ray asked.

"The client meeting took an hour, and the call with my son took ten minutes."

"Okay," Ray said. *"How was the rest of your day?"*

"It was fine," I said. "I had another meeting with a client that went really well, I spent some quality time with Brian, and I had a good workout."

"Okay. Well, if you removed those two challenging circumstances, what score would you have given your day?"

"I'm not sure. Maybe a 1.6? Wait, are you suggesting that if I took the average of the Minutes I spent in Bucket One compared to the ones I spent in Bucket Three, my overall score wouldn't be as terrible?"

"That's exactly what I'm saying."

"But what about the way those Bucket Three Minutes affected all my other Minutes? Sure, the phone call with my son was only ten minutes, but it bothered me for the rest of the day. It's still bothering me!"

Ray didn't respond right away. Eventually he said, *"Karen, I've got good news and bad news. The bad news is that you're talking right now with a hyper-analytic person. Numbers matter more to me than feelings. So…so what if you didn't feel good? Weren't you making great decisions? I mean, I personally hate more than half of my workouts, but that doesn't make them bad decisions. Despite the small amount of time you spent feeling aggravated, I'd say the majority of your Minutes were still going into Bucket One."*

He looked down from the Zoom cam for a moment and scribbled something on a piece of paper. *"That means the good news is that, by my calculations, even if all the neutral minutes of your day were scored as a 2, a more accurate score for your day would be 1.65."*

I thought about this for a while. Here I was thinking that I'd spent my whole day in Bucket Three and Ray was telling me that no, in fact, everything was mostly fine. The majority of my Minutes were still going into Bucket One.

The more I considered his perspective, the more I realized he was right. I had been too hard on myself, doubting my ability to allocate my Minutes to Bucket One, even though I was still doing a good job overall. I had lost faith in myself, even when my actions showed I was still deserving of my own trust.

Even though I wasn't feeling fully engaged, I still made conscious decisions to spend my time appropriately. I wasn't in despair—and I wasn't relinquishing my commitment. I was simply feeling down because *some* of my time went toward Bucket Three activities. Having some Bucket Three Minutes didn't mean that all of my time was poorly spent—even if it did make it harder to enjoy the time I allocated to Bucket One.

As Ray and I discussed how we evaluated our Minutes, we came to a simple conclusion: if Minutes are like currency, we should treat them as such. Each Minute is equally valuable, just like each dollar. What matters most is how you choose to spend those Minutes, regardless of how you feel about your decision.

If you impulsively invest a dollar in a trendy stock and the company goes bankrupt, your initial feeling about the investment doesn't matter; it likely wasn't a wise decision. However, if you invest that same dollar after carefully researching various options such as ETFs, bonds, or high-yield savings accounts, the chances are that your money is relatively secure, and you've made a sound choice—even if it's not as thrilling as investing in a hot stock.

Eventually, when you look back at your investment decisions years down the road, how will you feel about the dollars saved versus the money wasted?

Our Minutes are like money. Making the right decisions with our time may not always be fun or exciting, but if we consciously put our Minutes in the right Buckets, we can be confident that we're investing our time wisely. In the future, we'll be thankful for the smart choices we made.

Remember, I said "the right Buckets" in plural. That's because Bucket Two is also important. If we try to spend all our Minutes in Bucket One, we might lose sight of what makes a Minute well spent. We need to appreciate the difference between a Minute in Bucket One and Bucket Three. Bucket Two is where we decide if it's worth investing our time in Bucket One activities. It's healthy to spend some time in Bucket Two, consciously deciding where our Minutes go. This way, no matter what we choose to do, we intentionally spend our Minutes on engaging and meaningful tasks.

The issue, as I've mentioned earlier, is that many individuals today spend an excessive amount of time in Bucket Two. Limbo is comfortable in its formlessness, like a rubber band that has been stretched so far that it loses its elasticity and shape. It requires minimal effort to spend Minutes in Bucket Two. However, none of that time allows you to actively engage with your purpose. It's a space that lends itself well to planning, but not to putting your plans in action. Bucket Two represents the point of decision—the fork in the road. If you set up camp right at the tip of the splitting path, you're not actually making progress in either direction.

The Bucket Journal combats the complacency of Bucket Two by bringing awareness to the Minutes spent there. It's acceptable to allocate some time to Bucket Two, as long as you do so mindfully. The value of these Minutes lies in how well you use them to reflect on your spending habits, planning out where you want to invest your future Minutes.

As John P. often says to me, "You can start your day in Bucket Two, but you sure as heck can't finish there. You *must* make a decision."

A tool like the Bucket Journal helps make that decision.

The Bucket Journal: How to Make Decisions *and Feel Good About Them!*

Using a tool like the Bucket Journal is similar to investing money in a reliable financial advisor. While you may never see the money spent on their fee again, their assistance increases your confidence in financial decisions. The Bucket Journal requires only a few Minutes of your time each day—Minutes that you won't get back—but because of that time invested, you'll feel much more secure about your time management decisions.

After my initial discussion with Ray, we brainstormed ideas for a more comprehensive tool that would account for all of the day's waking Minutes. We delved deep into the details, and I mean really deep.

Ray explained his new ideas like this: "Assuming we get eight hours of sleep each night, that leaves us with sixteen waking hours to make decisions. Some of the most crucial decisions for our well-being revolve around our physical activity and diet. Therefore, we'll evaluate our Minute-spending decisions in relation to our food choices and daily step count. When it comes to the hours in our day, we're either fully engaged, not thinking about them, or despising every Minute of them. That's Bucket One, Two, or Three, respectively.

"By considering these factors, we can create a more comprehensive formula that takes into account not only our mental and emotional engagement but also our physical well-being. This holistic approach will provide a more accurate representation of how we're spending our Minutes and help us make better decisions to optimize our time and overall health."

For those who are hyper-analytical like Ray and wish to incorporate a similar approach to the Bucket Journal as he has, here's the formula he's shared that you can integrate into your evening journaling routine:

$$(((\text{Start-of-Day Score} + \text{End-of-Day Score}) / 2) + \text{Diet Score} + \text{Movement Score}) / 3$$

Let's break down the components of this formula:

Start-of-Day Score: How you feel at the beginning of the day, rated on a scale of 1 to 3.

End-of-Day Score: How you feel at the end of the day, rated on a scale of 1 to 3.

Diet Score: A score based on your food choices throughout the day, rated on a scale of 1 to 3, with healthier choices receiving a higher score.

Movement Score: A score based on your physical activity and step count, rated on a scale of 1 to 3, with more movement resulting in a higher score.

While Ray's comprehensive formula offers a detailed approach to evaluating your day, it's important to remember that the essence of the Bucket Journal isn't the score itself. Instead, it's about bringing awareness to the time you spend in Bucket Two while acknowledging the slippery slope that can lead to Bucket Three. It's a practice of dedicating time to rebuilding trust in yourself.

Though Ray religiously deploys his formula each day, do I follow the same plan? No, I don't. While I find it intriguing, I'm not as concerned with the accuracy of my score. The essence of the Bucket Journal isn't the score itself. Instead, it's about bringing awareness to the time I spend in Bucket Two while acknowledging the slippery slope that can lead to Bucket Three. It's a practice of dedicating time to rebuilding trust in myself.

Remember, we want to put Minutes into Bucket Two so we can maximize the amount we spend in Bucket One. The difference between a score of 1.5 and 1.556 isn't as important as knowing that our Minutes are mostly going into Bucket One, with some room for improvement.

While optimizing time allocations across the buckets, it's essential to consider some key perspectives. I want to share a few crucial insights from my discussions with Ray that are worth keeping in mind:

1. **Distinguishing between decisions and feelings**
   - I may dread a workout, procrastinate before starting, and even complain throughout the entire process, but I rarely regret it once it's finished. (Even in cases where I do, it's usually because I've pulled a muscle, not because of the workout itself.)
   - Although I may not enjoy the exercise in the moment, I'm still actively engaged with my physical well-being, which makes the workout a good decision.
   - In my view, exercise is always a 1 and never a 3. If it's beneficial for the body, then it's a wise choice. Conversely, if it's not healthy for the body, then it's probably not the best decision.

2. **Assessing feelings at the beginning and end of the day**
   - I used to leave evaluation time for the end of each day. Now, I assess how I feel both at the beginning and end of the day.
   - This approach allows me to observe any shifts in my sense of engagement throughout the day.

- If one score differs significantly from the other, I can examine my day more closely to determine whether one or two specific events are heavily influencing my score, or if my End-of-Day Score truly reflects how I feel.

3. **The importance of consistent journaling**
   - Ray has confided in me that he doesn't particularly enjoy journaling. However, that doesn't deter him from responding to a few questions about his day when he calculates his score.
   - Some of the questions he addresses in his version of a "journal" are:
     - ✓ How do I feel about my day?
     - ✓ Have I experienced this feeling before? If so, when? If not, what are my thoughts on this new feeling?
     - ✓ What actions must I take tomorrow to allocate more Minutes to Bucket One?
     - ✓ Is there a change I need to make? If so, what is it?

If you're uncertain about where you spend your Minutes each day, the Bucket Journal can help you gain clarity. Not knowing where your Minutes are going is unfair to yourself. You have the right to know where things are headed. You deserve that trust!

When you encounter a score of 2 or higher on any given day, don't panic. Take a moment to reflect on your experiences. Remind yourself of your purpose and contemplate what you can do tomorrow to better align your time spent with those goals. If a change is required, commit to making it happen. Above all, be kind to yourself. A bad day isn't the end of the world. The goal isn't to achieve perfection. It's simply to acknowledge that you possess the capability to step into Bucket Two and swiftly step back out again.

If you can accomplish this, you're well on your way to mastering Three Bucket Leadership. You're taking the appropriate steps to regain trust in yourself, which in turn allows you to demonstrate your trustworthiness to the people on your team who rely on your support.

The Bucket Journal is a powerful tool for self-reflection and time management. By dedicating a few Minutes each day to evaluate your experiences and decisions, you can gain a clearer understanding of where your time is being spent and make conscious choices to align your actions with your purpose. Remember, the key is to be mindful of the time you spend in Bucket Two and to take action when necessary to avoid slipping into Bucket Three.

As you embark on your journey with the Bucket Journal, be patient with yourself and celebrate the small victories along the way. Every day presents a new opportunity to invest your Minutes wisely and move closer to becoming the best version of yourself. So, grab a pen and paper, or download the app when it becomes available, and start taking control of your time today. Your future self will thank you for the trust you're building and the purposeful life you're creating, one Minute at a time.

CHAPTER 9

The Path to Purpose

As my boys grew up, I made it my mission to teach them to make good decisions. Sure, I covered the basics, like showing them right from wrong, but I wanted to go deeper. I wanted to help them figure out their purposes in life so they could pursue them with unwavering determination. I tried to be as involved as possible, helping them explore what made them tick. I wanted nothing more than to see my boys living full, honest, and meaningful lives.

One of my biggest worries was that the world would derail my kids away from what really mattered to them. I wanted to be their cheerleader, but not for typical goals like high salaries, fancy titles, or impressive degrees. What I really cared about was seeing them spend as much time as possible doing whatever lit them up inside. It didn't matter to me if they ended up as hotshot executives, electricians, or garbage collectors. As long as they were happy, healthy, and engaged, I was all for it.

From the moment my firstborn, Rory, entered the world, he had a clear sense of purpose. Even as a tiny baby, he approached every task with an astonishing level of determination, seemingly eager to grow up and take on the world. He hit milestones early—he crawled, walked, and talked long before his peers. He even started reading before most kids his age. And while I may not have taken it too seriously at the time, he had his career path all mapped out by the tender age of three.

Most toddlers want to be firefighters, police officers, veterinarians, astronauts, or teachers. Some want to follow in their parents' footsteps. Well, not my son. His journey started with a rather unfortunate incident that led him to his unexpected childhood hero—his podiatrist. This chance encounter sparked a fascination that would ultimately shape his future and set him on a journey to discover his true calling.

One spring morning, my two boys, Rory and Liam, were in the front of the house playing with some neighborhood friends. I was in the kitchen with a cup of tea, listening to giggles and squeals drifting in through the open window. Suddenly, a scream pierced the air, a sound so shrill and intense that it sent shivers down my spine. Instantly, I knew it belonged to one of my sons. Before I could even process what was happening, I leapt from my chair, propelled by an instinctive urge to protect and comfort my child.

I found Rory tangled up in a neighbor's garden hose, screaming at the top of his lungs. The concrete stairs next to him had a bloodstain that matched a gaping wound on his leg. The bone in his shin looked...wrong. I could tell it was broken at just a glance. I made a conscious effort not to wince, scooped up my baby, and headed straight to the car. While strapping Rory in the booster seat, Brian (alerted by the commotion) gathered up Liam and deposited him in the car seat next to his screaming brother. We took off toward the hospital.

Now, I have an...issue...with leg injuries. Call it a leftover phobia from my own accident. I tried my best to stay calm as I carried my three-year-old into the emergency room, but I was terrified. I thought for sure the doctor was going to suggest we cut Rory's leg off. I could hardly control my shaking. Rory, ever observant even at his age, could sense my fear. And if Mom is scared, he should be too, right? So, we cried together while we waited for the doctor to see us.

A few hours later, we learned Rory had a spiral fracture in his tibia. This meant his bone was broken *and* a little twisted, which was problematic for a three-year-old boy with plenty of growing to do. The injury was dangerously close to the growth plate in his leg and required expert care, beyond what the hospital could provide. The emergency room doctor recommended we follow up with a pediatric podiatrist, so we booked an appointment for the following week.

After a week of being cooped up on the living room couch, Rory was practically bouncing off the walls. I wasn't faring much better myself. Without knowing for sure what would happen next, I'd spent the week resisting the urge to smother those five tiny toes with goodbye kisses. As if my nerves weren't already frayed enough, when we finally stepped into the podiatrist's office, we were greeted by a man who looked like he had just come fresh from his high school graduation. I felt so anxious for a moment, I nearly turned and marched back to the lobby to demand a more experienced doctor. But then I saw how he treated my son.

In no time at all, Rory and the podiatrist were cracking jokes, laughing, and having an absolute blast together. The doctor handled my anxiety and Rory's discomfort like a seasoned pro. He assured me that he knew precisely how to treat my son's injury and expressed confidence that we'd have his leg back to normal in no time—definitely no amputation. It was clear this doctor lived a life of passion and purpose, and his enthusiasm was infectious.

I walked out of the office feeling relieved about our visit, and Rory left sporting a seriously cool Ninja Turtles leg cast. Wins all around!

We visited the podiatrist weekly for almost four months, and Rory always looked forward to the appointment. Most kids his age loved dinosaurs and rocket ships, but Rory was all about feet, toes, and bones. He spent most nights playing doctor, wrapping towels around his brother's leg in makeshift casts. The kid was All In on podiatry.

At his final appointment, I left Rory and his father behind in the doctor's exam room while I paid up at the front desk. Just as I handed the check to the clerk, Rory came bounding through the reception doors and crashed right into my legs. Brian and the doctor followed behind.

"Mom, I know what I want to be when I grow up!"

"You do? What's that, honey?" I asked, recording the payment in my checkbook.

"I'm going to be a pod-it-trist!" he said, beaming.

The other parents in the waiting room laughed, but Rory was serious. I looked up at the doctor.

"Did you have something to do with this?"

The doctor laughed and held up his hands in surrender. "He's a natural, Mrs. Gilhooly."

I looked back at my little boy. "Well, Rory, we'd better get to studying, then. You've got a looooong road ahead!"

The doctor was right about Rory—he *was* a natural. Over the years, I've watched him demonstrate skills only mastered by the best doctors in the world. He is extremely empathetic, so in tune with other people's emotions he can walk up to someone on the opposite side of a room and dive headfirst into a discussion about their state of mind. His emotional intelligence, passion, and determination stayed with him all the way into adulthood. It wasn't an Easy Road for Rory to follow, but he had the drive, and he had his family's support. Today, he *is* a podiatrist, and he's the best one I've ever seen. (Okay, I might be *a little* biased, but that doesn't mean I'm wrong!)

Forging Forward: Finding the Perfect Path

Liam, my second-born son, had a harder time finding his purpose. From a young age, Liam exhibited a contrarian nature, always questioning the status quo and seeking truth through arguments and debates. He thrived on challenging his father's opinions and never accepted "because I told you so" as a valid reason for anything. As a contrarian myself, I loved engaging Liam in these endless discussions, particularly when it came to important decisions in his life. My own childhood experiences taught me the significance of understanding the rationale behind a decision, and I made sure to instill the importance of defending one's point of view in Liam—despite the amount of energy needed to accomplish this.

After years of playing rousing games of verbal tennis with him, I realized Liam's true calling was to challenge and enlighten those around him. Together, we explored various career paths that could align with his skills and passions. We researched careers in teaching, philosophy, politics, and law. After graduating from high school, Liam surprised everyone by announcing his plans to become an inventor or business entrepreneur, rejecting the more conventional options we'd covered in the past.

Although I believed he would excel in either role, I still encouraged him to pursue an undergraduate degree. It wasn't because I thought he'd fail in his pursuit—it was quite the opposite, actually. I wanted him to have a backup plan in case he discovered these options didn't engage him enough. I wanted him to have a safety net in case he found himself trapped in Bucket Three. I hoped Liam would consider attending law school to refine his debating skills, but ever confident in his abilities, he declined.

As Liam approached his final year of undergraduate studies, the pressures of adulthood began to weigh on him, and our conversations shifted to more practical career choices. He contemplated becoming a teacher, acknowledging that it could be a good match for him. However, I had a nagging thought he might struggle on this path. While Liam's rebellious nature and love for debate could bring a fresh perspective to the classroom, the structured nature of the curriculum and educational standards might prove frustrating for someone so motivated to challenge the status quo. Moreover, the repetitive nature of teaching might not fully satisfy Liam's thirst for knowledge, nor his desire for a constant challenge.

I wasn't blind to the fact that these were the same thoughts my high school counselor expressed to me all those years ago. She also worried I wouldn't find teaching challenging enough. I had a new perspective on her advice, and while I do still wonder what kind of life I could have led as a teacher, I also have a new appreciation for her advice. To find fulfillment, my counselor believed I needed a profession that would force me to continuously evolve. I felt the same about Liam.

I chose to let my concerns about a teaching career simmer without sharing them with Liam. I knew whatever career he chose would depend on his willingness to adapt to challenges, limitations, and accomplishments. He would find a way to incorporate his unique skills and passion into whatever he decided. Within a few weeks, the teaching prospect left the list of potential paths, leaving Liam once again without clear direction.

As the holiday break approached, I noticed a change in Liam's demeanor. He seemed more pensive than usual, often lost in thought. I wondered what was going through his mind, but I knew better than to pry. Liam had always been the type to come to me when he was ready to talk.

One evening, while I was preparing dinner, Liam walked into the kitchen with a determined look on his face. "Mom, we need to talk," he said, his voice filled with a seriousness I hadn't heard before.

"Okay, honey, what's up?" I replied, trying for a light tone despite the growing concern in my heart.

"No, Mom. I need to talk about something important. We need to have the kind of talk where we sit on the couch and look at each other."

His words sent a chill down my spine. My mind raced with possibilities. Was he in trouble? Was he going to drop out of school? I wrung my shaking hands and turned off the stove.

As we settled onto the couch, facing each other, I could see a stolid intensity in Liam's eyes. He took a deep breath, as if gathering his courage, and then spoke the words that would change everything.

"Mom, you were right."

I blinked, unsure if I had heard him correctly. Liam, my obstinate son, admitting that I was right about *anything*? It seemed too good to be true.

"I'm sorry, can you repeat that?" I asked, a smirk threatening to break free from the corner of my mouth.

Liam smiled, a hint of mischief in his eyes. "You were right, Mom. I need to go to law school."

Relief washed over me, followed by a surge of pride. My son, who had always been so adamant about forging his own path, had come to this decision on his own. I felt a sense of validation, knowing the seeds I had planted over the years had finally taken root.

But Liam wasn't finished. "There's a small catch, though," he continued, his expression growing serious once more. "I want to get my MBA after my JD degree."

For those unfamiliar with the world of law school, law students typically pursue their Juris Doctor (JD) degree before any other because it's required to practice law in the United States. It's not common for lawyers (or other professionals) to earn an MBA as well.

Liam continued, "That way, if I decide to pursue a career in law, I'll have the business degree to back me up. If I decide to go into business, I'll have the legal skills to navigate the process. Either way, I win. What do you think?"

I sat there for a moment, taking in the magnitude of his words. My son had always been so resistant to structure and conformity and was now embracing a path that would require years of head-down, hard-pressed work. As I looked at him, my heart flooded with a profound admiration for the person he had grown into.

"Liam," I said, my voice thick with emotion, "I think that's a brilliant plan. It won't be easy, but if anyone can do it, it's you. I'm so proud of you for coming to this decision on your own."

Liam's face lit up, and he leaned forward to give me a hug. As I held him close, I couldn't help but marvel at the journey to this moment. Liam, who had always marched to the beat of his own drum, was now ready to take on the world on his own terms. And I couldn't wait to see where his path would lead him.

As he embarked on his journey to obtain his JD and MBA, I watched with a mixture of pride and amazement. The once rebellious and stubborn child transformed into a determined and focused young man, ready to take on the challenges of adulthood. Despite the grueling schedule, Liam never wavered in his commitment. He excelled in his classes, finding new ways to challenge his intellect and think outside the box. His contrarian nature, once a source of frustration, now served him well as he challenged conventional wisdom and proposed innovative solutions to complex problems.

Upon graduation, Liam accepted a position at a boutique law firm in Madison, Wisconsin. The opportunity to work closely with clients and make a tangible difference in their lives was what attracted him to the work. Liam's tasks at the firm vary and always prove challenging—just as he had hoped. His unique blend of legal expertise and business acumen have made him a valuable asset to his firm and his clients.

My boys' paths may look completely different, but they both reached their ultimate destination: an engaging life. Rory, who knew his path from a young age and pursued it with unwavering determination, blossomed into a skilled podiatrist dedicated to helping others heal. His story exemplifies the power of having a clear purpose and the courage to follow it.

Liam, on the other hand, took a different yet equally inspiring route. From the inquisitive child who questioned everything to the accomplished professional who uses his unique perspective to make a difference, Liam remained true to himself. His journey testifies to the importance of embracing one's individuality and forging one's own way.

Today, I look at my boys and know they've both found their places in the world. They're living life on their own terms. They've discovered the perfect personal crossroads where their skills, passions, and values intersect. Rory and Liam are shining examples of what it means to live a life of purpose, fulfillment, and authentic engagement. They live Bucket One lives.

As a parent, I practiced Three Bucket Leadership with my kids the same as I do with my work teams. The leadership skills needed to guide Minutes into Bucket One are universal—they're not limited to parents, soccer coaches, or spiritual guides. Three Bucket Leaders empower people to find purpose, and they show people how to prioritize spending their time on what matters to them.

However, discovering one's purpose isn't always as straightforward as it was for Rory. Many people, like Liam, may need to explore various paths and experiences before finding their true calling. As a Three Bucket Leader, your job is to guide them through this process, offering strategies to help them gain direction and stay on the Hard Road.

Mapping Out a Path: The Power of Pros and Cons Lists

There is a simple yet powerful tool you can use to help determine anyone's purpose: the pros and cons list. By encouraging a person to reflect on their past experiences and current interests, you can help them identify patterns and themes that point toward their unique purpose. Let's explore how this tool can be used effectively in a leadership context.

Step 1: Reflect on past experiences

Encourage the individual to create a list of their past jobs, roles, or experiences. For each item on the list, have them write down the pros and cons of that particular experience. Prompt them to consider questions such as:

- What did you enjoy about this role?
- What did you find challenging or frustrating?
- What skills or strengths did you utilize in this position?
- What aspects of the job aligned with your values?

Step 2: Identify patterns and themes

Once the individual has completed their list, help them analyze the information to identify any recurring themes or patterns. Look for commonalities among the pros and cons across different experiences. Ask questions like:

- What characteristics do the enjoyable aspects of your experiences share?
- Are there any skills or strengths that consistently emerge in roles you found fulfilling?
- Do you notice any values or priorities that are present in the experiences you enjoyed most?

Step 3: Explore current interests and passions

Next, have the individual create a new list focusing on their current interests, hobbies, and passions. Encourage them to write down the activities they enjoy outside of work and the pros and cons associated with each. Consider questions such as:

- What do you spend your free time on?
- What aspects of these activities do you find most engaging or rewarding?
- Are there any skills or strengths you utilize in these pursuits?
- How do these activities align with your values or priorities?

Step 4: Synthesize the information

Help the individual review both lists and identify any connections or overlaps between their past experiences and current interests. Look for themes that emerge across both lists, as these may point toward their unique purpose or calling. Ask questions like:

- Are there any similarities between the enjoyable aspects of your past experiences and your current interests?
- Do you notice any skills or strengths that are present in both your work and personal pursuits?
- Are there any values or priorities that consistently emerge across both lists?

Step 5: Develop an action plan

Once the individual has identified potential areas of purpose or passion, work with them to create an action plan for pursuing these interests. This may involve:

- Researching potential career paths or roles that align with their identified purpose

- Seeking out educational or training opportunities to develop relevant skills
- Connecting with individuals who are already working in fields of interest
- Setting short-term and long-term goals to guide their journey toward their purpose

By breaking down the pros and cons list process into these five steps, individuals can more effectively use this tool to gain clarity on their unique purpose and develop a road map for pursuing a life of authentic engagement. As a Three Bucket Leader, your role is to guide them through this process, offer support and encouragement, and help them navigate any challenges that may arise along the way.

Remember, discovering one's purpose is a journey, and it may take time and exploration to find the right path. By empowering individuals to reflect on their experiences, interests, and values, you can help them move closer to a life that truly resonates with their authentic selves. The pros and cons list is a valuable tool in this process, providing a framework for self-discovery and a foundation for purposeful action.

Guiding with Purpose: A Three Bucket Leader's Approach

As a Three Bucket Leader, you're bound to come across people on your team who still don't know their purpose. As we saw with Allen C. Johnson, they move through the ranks at their job and end up with you, but not because they're perfectly aligned with their position—they're just not misaligned enough to be fired or motivated to quit. So, what do you do with them?

What do a firefighter, a car salesperson, and a teacher have in common?

It's not about what they have in common—it's about *who* they have in common.

Jason started his career as a volunteer firefighter, but the danger and demands of the job pushed him away. The next job he found was a commission-based gig at the local used car dealership, but that didn't feel like it fit his purpose either. He moved on to be a substitute teacher, and though he liked the work for a while, that job eventually proved a poor use of his Minutes as well.

Now, here's the kicker. Jason finally landed a job working as an accounting clerk for one of my clients—we'll call her Sarah—and, unfortunately, his job turned out to be as uninspiring as the rest. The poor man felt completely adrift, like he was ready to throw in the towel altogether. So, what did my client decide to do next? She got to work.

After a bit of prodding, Sarah realized it was time to help Jason figure out his next steps. He had been wandering aimlessly for so long, without any clear sense of purpose, that even a glimmer of hope for forward momentum would light him up. I assured Sarah that even if Jason's next move came in the form of a resignation letter, those remaining two weeks would be filled with productivity and progress rather than a drain on everyone's energy. It was an opportunity to reignite Jason's spark and help him find his way, no matter where his path led next.

How did Sarah help Jason identify his next move? Well, she told him to start a pros and cons list. She instructed him to write down what he liked and disliked about each job in his career. A few days later, when they examined Jason's job characteristics, one common denominator stood out against each role: the chance to help people. Now, I know this might sound a bit broad at first glance, but this desire to make a positive difference in others' lives is what motivated Jason. It was the core of what gave his work a sense of purpose.

Armed with this knowledge, Sarah now faced the task of helping Jason connect that purpose to an environment that would genuinely engage him. To accomplish this, she needed Jason to create a fresh list. She told him to jot down the pros and cons of all the activities he pursued outside of work. What did he spend his time on outside of work? What aspects of these activities did he find enjoyable? What parts did he find less appealing or even off-putting?

From this new list, Sarah discovered that Jason spent a lot of time at the gym. More notably, he *loved* his time at the gym. Everything about it. Not only did he enjoy working on himself, but he also loved helping other people tweak their workouts, celebrate their sets, and find new ways to improve. Bingo.

"Maybe," Sarah suggested, "you'd enjoy being a personal trainer." He loved the idea. Except…there were some obstacles.

Becoming a personal trainer requires training, certifications, and a certain number of hours of experience with clients under supervision. This wasn't a switch Jason could make overnight. Not to mention the fact that Sarah was effectively suggesting a path that would take Jason *away* from her company. Now she had to work out a pair of transition plans. One for him, and one for herself.

It was a Hard Road ahead for both of them.

Together, the two crafted plans to suit both their needs. They gave Jason the time he needed to pursue his new educational goals, while also providing Sarah with a reasonable timeline to find a great replacement. But here's the fascinating part: by empowering Jason to chase after his true passions, Sarah stumbled upon an unexpected benefit.

Even though Jason was on his way out the door, the quality of his work skyrocketed. His output became more accurate, timely, and efficient than ever before. It was like watching a whole new Jason emerge, and he hadn't even landed his dream job yet! Just the mere act of taking steps toward his true calling was enough to ignite his engagement levels. In other words, while he may not have been in his ideal role just yet, more of his Minutes found their way into Bucket One.

As Jason's enthusiasm grew, it rippled out toward those around him, particularly his replacement. In the months leading up to his departure from Sarah's team, a new hire came on board to take over his responsibilities. During the transition period, Jason trained and mentored her. The new hire appreciated the chance to learn from someone who was leaving the position for personal growth reasons rather than any negativity toward the company. Jason, in turn, felt a sense of satisfaction knowing that he was leaving the organization on positive terms and with a capable successor in place. By the time he bid his final farewell to the company, everyone involved found themselves squarely in Bucket One.

All because he took the time to compile a couple of pros and cons lists.

CHAPTER 10

The Courage to Engage

The way you spend your time boils down to the way you make your decisions. When you're fully engaged, you make better choices about how to allocate your time, energy, and financial resources. While the concept of aligning your decisions with your purpose sounds appealing, the reality is that most of us struggle to consistently make great choices.

To better understand this challenge, let's revisit the Three Buckets concept. Bucket One represents time spent on activities that align with your purpose and bring you fulfillment. Bucket Two represents time spent on necessary tasks that may not be directly related to your purpose but still support your overall well-being and engagement. Bucket Three represents time spent on activities that drain your energy, and this wasted time does nothing for your overall progress in life.

Making great decisions becomes more manageable when your job aligns with your purpose. For instance, if your purpose is to help others lead healthier lives, a job as a wellness coach or nutritionist would provide ample opportunities to spend Minutes in Bucket One. On the other hand, if your purpose is to bring laughter and joy to others, working on a factory line won't provide you with many opportunities to connect with people the way you'd like. Similarly, if you find fulfillment in creating art, be it through writing, painting, composing music, or crafting pottery, a job as a data analyst won't give you the chance to spend Minutes in Bucket One. When your purpose and your job are misaligned, every decision you make feels off-kilter, as if you're constantly swimming against the current.

Even when people have a clear understanding of their purpose, it doesn't necessarily mean their decisions become effortless. They must consciously choose to use their purpose as a guiding light, a North Star, even when it leads down a path of difficult choices.

Engaging with the world, your job, the people you love, and your daily life requires a great deal of courage. Living a Bucket One life demands bravery because you must dedicate all of your Minutes to making sound decisions. You must push through the exhaustion, the fear, and the temptation to take the Easy Road. Bucket Two also calls for courage, as it requires you to reflect on your current choices and confront the reality of your situation, which can be a challenging—even uncomfortable—process. Even a Bucket Three existence necessitates courage, since escaping Bucket Three means admitting it's time for a change and finding strength to take action.

My personal journey exemplifies the courage it takes to make a significant life change in pursuit of a more fulfilling existence. The Three Bucket Leader model inspired me to make the most courageous decision of my life. After watching my husband's video and confronting my own ghost, I faced a difficult choice. I realized that if I continued along the path I was on, I would never find my way back to Bucket One. Despite the temptation to resist change and pretend I hadn't seen the video, a louder, more insistent voice within me screamed it was too late to turn back. If I didn't make a bold decision right then, I would never help anyone else make great decisions again.

I saw the video on a Saturday. On Monday, I left my job.

Over the weekend, I acknowledged my despair head-on. I had hit rock bottom, and there was no turning back. Months earlier, my longtime boss and mentor had retired, leaving me without the guidance I had relied on for so long. I was now a solo act, making a huge decision with immense implications for myself, my family, and my team.

My new manager, despite not knowing me well, recognized the tremendous pressure I had been under before he joined the organization. In discussing my departure, he was gracious and kind. In fact, we were both relieved. The two of us worked out a transition plan that felt fair on both sides, and I finally saw the first few glimmers of hope reappear in my life.

When I shared the decision with my husband, he wasn't particularly shocked to discover I'd reached my limit. However, what caught him off guard was my backup plan—or lack thereof.

"This isn't like you, Karen," he said. "You're normally ten steps ahead of the game. What are you going to do instead? Do you have another job lined up you haven't told me about?"

"No," I said quietly, but then I repeated it louder, solidifying my own resolve. "No, no, I don't. I don't have anything lined up. But it doesn't matter. I don't know what I want to do next—but I'm absolutely certain I'm not where I need to be. I haven't been for a long time. I know it, and you know it too."

"Okay, Karen," he said, putting his head in his hands. "We'll figure it out. It's clear that you haven't been in a good place for some time now. We'll miss the money, but if this is what it takes to bring back the 'happy Karen' we all know and love, then I'm All In. We'll make it work."

Next, I had to announce my resignation to my team, which was almost harder than the talk with my family. After all my years of pushing Three Bucket Leadership, promoting engagement, and promising to help everyone stay aligned, I had to admit I'd failed at following my own system. I felt like a hypocrite.

My team admitted they'd noticed a change in my behavior over the past few months, but they didn't realize how far I'd fallen. Once they understood the extent of my disengagement, they were incredibly supportive. I felt an overwhelming sense of love and understanding from the entire team, from the most junior person to my most trusted, experienced manager. Their reaction told me they didn't see me as a hypocrite—instead, they saw me as a human. And they saw that if this could happen to me, it could happen to anyone.

One of the great outcomes of this situation was the reinforcement of the Bucket theory. Specifically, it showed me the value of redemption. There was no shame in my failure; the only disgrace would be failing to learn from it. This experience reminded me that everyone has the capacity to overcome setbacks and grow stronger, wiser, and more resilient. It also emphasized the importance of creating a supportive environment, where people feel safe to share their struggles and receive the help they need to get back on track.

As I embarked on my journey to reengage with my purpose, I felt a mix of emotions. I felt certain that it was time for a new start, and that certainty lasted until my very last day with the company. On that final morning, as I got out of bed and looked out my window, something changed. Working from my

Florida home, I watched the rising sun bathe the palm trees in a golden glow. Despite the beauty, I felt empty. I realized I was leaving my purpose behind, letting it dry up and vanish like the morning dew on my lawn.

The weight of my decision hit me hard, and I questioned whether I'd made the right choice. The realization that I was walking away from a job that had given my life meaning and direction overwhelmed me, leaving me emotionally raw and vulnerable.

This feeling—this all-consuming terror—felt eerily familiar, like encountering a stranger from my past. The ache in my chest and the heaviness in my stomach were unmistakable. It was the unwelcome return of a sensation I swore I would never experience again. At that moment, I realized I had come full circle, back to the place I thought I'd left behind for good. Rock bottom had reared its ugly head once again.

Surprisingly, this realization didn't discourage me. As I emptied myself of tears, I also released all my fears, regrets, and apprehension. My worries crumbled away, replaced by a solid resolve. I knew exactly why I left—I did it because I was no longer fully engaged with life. With that realization, I knew that every Minute I spent at that job was a Minute wasted. It was time to reengage, and although I didn't know what that looked like yet, I had faith I would find my way. I always had, and I always will.

Finding True North

My first week of unemployment was filled with aimless wandering. I meandered around the house, watering plants, straightening paintings, folding and unfolding blankets. I spent hours on the phone with old friends and colleagues, seeking their guidance and support. Even though I didn't have a solid plan to fulfill my purpose yet, I could feel it bubbling up inside me. I knew it was only a matter of time before the next stop on my journey would become clear, pointing me in the direction of my true calling.

"You should write a book," my husband said to me over dinner one night.

"Yeah, I probably could write a book," I said with a laugh. "I mean, considering all the people out there who are in the same situation I was in…so many people hate their jobs but don't know how to change their circumstances. They are trapped by their own inertia."

Brian nodded.

"And it's destroying them," I continued, "just like it nearly destroyed me. Maybe I can do something to help. Just because I'm not in banking anymore doesn't mean I can't do anything. I still have the power to help people engage with their lives."

I pondered the idea for a moment. Brian was right—even in the few calls I'd had the past week, most if not all the people I spoke to admitted they were somewhat envious of me. They longed for the conviction to start off on their own new journey, to discover their true purpose. Yet I understood that without a catalyst, without something to spur them into action, they would remain captive.

"You know," I joked, "if I put my mind to it, I could probably write it in a week."

Now it was his turn to laugh. "Okay, Karen. You may have lost your job, but you definitely haven't lost your ability to exaggerate. I look forward to reading the manuscript next week."

The next day, I began working on my book. I managed to complete the introduction and the first chapter, though they differed from what appears in the beginning of the book now. However, before I could make further progress, my purpose came calling, and I discovered a new direction that would shape the next leg of my journey.

I put my book on hold to concentrate on a new business venture—True North Collaboration. I aimed to create an organization where I could fulfill my calling by helping others do the same. After years of being known in my structured career as "the engagement expert," I wanted to bring my skills to places where there weren't people like me focusing on engagement. I hoped to find individuals spending their Minutes in the wrong Bucket and teach them how to discover their guiding light... their True North.

Since starting this new venture, I've witnessed firsthand how few people truly enjoy their work. I've realized there are vast numbers of people who aren't engaged. They're asleep at the wheel, and regardless of their immense potential to make an impact on the world, they can't seem to wake up and make the right decisions. Even when they become aware of how many Minutes they've spent in Bucket Three, they struggle to choose a new strategy to engage.

"I can't just quit my job, Karen. I have a family to support and bills to pay."

"I'm so close to retirement. If I leave now, I'll lose my pension."

"I'm saving for retirement, and I'm not fully vested yet. I can't go anywhere for another year or two."

And I say the same thing to every person who brings me their (very real and very formidable) excuses: "This choice belongs to you. You may not be able to change your job, but you can certainly change how you engage with it."

We don't own much in this world, but we do own our Minutes. We also own how we think about the world around us. If we're not using our perspectives to make a more meaningful difference in our lives, or the lives of people we love, what are we doing?

Yes, money might be tight for a while. But if you're currently earning a healthy salary, it's likely you'll reach that level of income again. Your skills, experience, and work ethic aren't tied to your job—they follow you wherever your journey leads. Your retirement account may receive smaller contributions, but there's no guarantee your Minutes will even carry you to retirement if you continue down this path. When you spend so much time disengaged with your life, you gamble with your own health and well-being.

Instead of focusing on what's stopping you from following your True North, what if you put those Minutes toward forging a new path? What if, instead of wallowing in Bucket Three, you decided to own your decisions and make them with Bucket One in mind? Your mindset, your decisions, and your courage are all tools at your disposal—they can either hold you back or propel you forward. Whatever you decide, the choice is yours and yours alone.

Making good decisions is ultimately up to you. I wanted to show my boys the way to a Bucket One life, but they had to make the right choices for themselves. As their mother, I hope they're making the best decisions every day (and I probably don't hear about their worst ones, anyway). In my work, I present my clients with the same path, hoping they'll take the first steps. But I can't force them to change how they spend their Minutes. My role is to be a guide, not a dictator.

You can't find someone else's purpose for them, no matter how much you might want to. Just like my high school counselor had no right to tell me not to teach, you can't tell another person what their purpose is. And since you can't determine their purpose, you also can't tell them the best way to spend their time. What you can do, though, is show them how fulfilling it is to be fully engaged. When you rediscover your own engagement and find your true calling, you can be a guiding light for others, inspiring them to start their own journey of self-discovery.

You can be a Three Bucket Leader.

One of the most rewarding aspects of my new career is making a difference in my clients' lives by simply investing my own Minutes in Bucket One. With every new person I meet, I showcase how engaging with purpose can turn the impossible into reality, opening up a world of opportunities they may have never considered before.

When I'm fully engaged with my life, my clients take notice. They see my engagement is genuine, not merely an act, and it sparks their curiosity. They grow eager to learn how they, too, can become fully engaged in their own lives.

"Karen, I've been thinking about what you said, and I realize I need to make a change. Can you help me figure out my next steps?"

"I never thought I could pursue my passion and make a living, but seeing how you've done it has inspired me to try. Where do I start?"

"Karen, I'm worried this business will never provide for me and my people. We've made a lot of progress and I'm thrilled that we're breaking even, but that's just not good enough. How can we dream bigger? I'm open to anything."

These questions didn't come from nowhere. They surfaced after months of developing relationships and building trust. The more I exemplify a Bucket One life, the more my clients clamor to understand how they can achieve the same level of fulfillment. As they begin to realign themselves with their true purpose—with what they deeply desire—they rediscover their untapped potential to live in Bucket One.

Learning to Fly (Again)

Starting a business from the ground up was no easy feat. There were days when I questioned my decision, yearning for the stability, comfort, and power my previous jobs provided. I gave up my influence, my network, my substantial paycheck, and my title, and for what? For the opportunity to forge my own path? Did I even truly want to carve out my own way?

That first year strained my resolve as much as it strained my bank account. Without the support of my husband, my sons, and my Bucket Journal, I might have given up. What kept me going during the toughest days was the expression on my clients' faces when we found the perfect match. I transformed teachers into salespeople and data analysts into creative geniuses. I turned teams upside down, revolutionized companies from within, and brought genuine change to the working world. Each new client had a unique story, and I helped them find their own happy ending.

Though I was poor in pennies, I was rich in Minutes. I loved it. I loved it all!

This newfound fulfillment was evident to those around me, even those from my past. About a year after starting True North, a trusted colleague from my banking days reached out to me. She wanted to know how I was doing, what I thought about my new business, and how I felt about my choice to leave the banking industry.

"Well, I'm not making any money, I'll tell you that much. But I'm having so much fun. I really am."

"That's great, Karen, but how long can you keep this up?"

"Who knows?" I said with a lighthearted laugh. My answer was true, but it didn't scare me. "These things take time. It's hard work building from the ground up. I've helped some incredible people find their true path and turned around teams at a few companies. I have total faith in what I'm doing. The money may or may not follow, but one thing is certain: I've never been happier."

"You're going to make it," she said.

"What makes you say that?"

"Well, I've been thinking a lot about you," she said, taking a deep breath, "and over the years, I've actually done a lot of research about personal success and engagement. Do you know the biggest predictor of success for people when they take a job?"

"No, what is it?"

"Whether they'd keep doing it for free."

That conversation lingered in my mind for weeks after we hung up. I continued to ask myself, "Would I do this for free?" The answer that consistently emerged was a resounding yes—a yes that resonated from the very core of my being. It was a yes that shook me to my bones and sent shivers down my spine. It was the most authentic yes I'd ever encountered, and the more I reflected on it, the more I realized it had been with me all along.

If I had to choose a term that best describes me, it would be something along the lines of an Engagement Teacher, Professor of Engagement, or Engagement Educator. No matter how you phrase it, I've been fulfilling this role my entire life. From the workbooks I insisted my cousins complete every Christmas, to the chore days I shared with my mom, to the lessons I imparted to my colleagues, friends, and sons, I engage with the world and share my energy with others. I encourage them to live their best lives, leading by example as a Three Bucket Leader.

Throughout this final chapter, we've explored the importance of making decisions that align with your purpose and the courage it takes to live a fully engaged life. By understanding the Three Bucket concept and making the decision to invest your Minutes in what engages you, you can unlock your true potential and create a valuable life for yourself.

As a Three Bucket Leader, you have the power to inspire change in others. By living your purpose and sharing your energy with the world, you can create a ripple effect of positive transformation that extends far beyond your own life. You can help your team, your business, and your family live more meaningful lives. When you lead by example, you show others what's possible and inspire them to pursue their own path to fulfillment.

So, my challenge to you is this: Embrace the courage to change. Make the decision to live a life true to your purpose. Choose to invest your Minutes in the people, activities, and experiences that bring you joy. The journey to a more engaging life starts with you, but for every Three Bucket Leader, there are countless people who learn from them.

The path to a purposeful life is not always easy, but it's always worth it. The journey of self-discovery that comes from living a Three Bucket life is never-ending. As you continue along your path, remember that every step, no matter how small, is a step toward the life you were always meant to live.

In summary, living a life aligned with your purpose requires courage, but the rewards are immeasurable. By making decisions that prioritize your engagement and investing your Minutes in Bucket One activities, you not only create a more fulfilling life for yourself but also inspire others to do the same. As a Three Bucket Leader, you have the power to create positive change in the world, one purposeful decision at a time.

Remember, your life is a tapestry woven by the threads of your decisions. Each choice you make, no matter how small, contributes to the overall picture of your existence. By having the courage to align your decisions with your purpose, you create a masterpiece that not only brings you joy and fulfillment but also inspires others to do the same.

Your legacy is defined not by the challenges you face, but by the courage you show in the face of those challenges. Embrace your purpose, trust in yourself, and make every Minute count. The world is waiting for you.

ACKNOWLEDGMENTS

I am deeply grateful to all the individual contributors, managers, and leaders whose passion and dedication create the incredible workplace experiences that shape our lives. My heartfelt thanks go to Ray Pendleton, Corrine Hickin, and Andy Earle for their collaborative efforts, and to my family for their patience and unwavering support. This book celebrates our shared journey and dreams.

ABOUT THE AUTHOR

Karen Gilhooly is an expert in employee engagement, leadership development, and organizational culture. As a senior executive with over twenty-five years of experience in the financial services industry, she has spearheaded culture transformations at Fortune 500 companies that resulted in higher retention, productivity, and profitability.

Frustrated by the failure of traditional engagement models, Karen developed the groundbreaking Three Bucket Leadership Framework to explain why employees become disengaged at work. Her framework redefines engagement as the willingness to spend one's most precious resources—time and attention—on work that provides meaning.

Karen now runs her own consulting firm specializing in leadership development and engagement strategies. When she isn't working, Karen enjoys spending time with her family, mentoring young women, and volunteering in her community.